Basic Concepts in Reading Instruction: A Programmed Approach

Second Edition

The Charles E. Merrill

COMPREHENSIVE READING PROGRAM

ARTHUR HEILMAN

Consulting Editor

Basic Concepts in Reading Instruction:

A Programmed Approach

Second Edition

Arnold Burron
University of Northern Colorado

Amos L. Claybaugh
University of Northern Colorado

Charles E. Merrill Publishing Company
A Bell & Howell Company
Columbus   Toronto   London   Sydney

The authors gratefully acknowledge the permission of Initial Teaching Alphabet Publications, Inc., 20 East 46th Street, New York, New York 10017, to reprint the Initial Teaching Alphabet.

LB 1050.37
B87
1977

Published by
Charles E. Merrill Publishing Company
A Bell & Howell Company
Columbus, Ohio 43216

International Standard Book Number: 0-675-08539-X

Library of Congress Catalog Card Number: 76-49381

1 2 3 4 5 6 7 — 82 81 80 79 78 77

Printed in the United States of America

Preface

Three questions were asked prior to the writing of this book:

1. Which concepts in the teaching of reading seem to be generally accepted as being fundamental for beginning students of reading instruction to learn?
2. What difficulties are commonly encountered by beginning students of reading instruction as they attempt to acquire these concepts?
3. What approach to presenting these concepts might minimize the difficulties encountered by beginning students of reading instruction?

An answer to the first question was sought through consultation with instructors of beginning reading courses and through a review of the literature directed toward the teaching of reading. A core of basic concepts emerged which appeared with consistency in both beginning reading courses and professional texts. Selected concepts from this core comprise the major portion of this book.

Beginning students of reading instruction offered answers to the second question. The concerns most frequently expressed were the following:

1. Beginning students need some kind of foundation, preview, or starting point to help them attain a fuller and more rapid understanding of class presentations and professional texts.
2. Intensive effort is required on the part of beginning students to identify and organize key concepts, even in the best of classes and with the best of texts.
3. Despite skillful guidance provided by competent instructors, it is difficult for beginning students to retain key concepts once they have been identified and organized.

The apparent effectiveness of programmed instruction in presenting factual material of an overview nature indicated one possible solution to the third question. The results of extensive testing of the lessons in this book suggested that programmed instruction could be one feasible response to the difficulties encountered by beginning students.

The questions and answers resulted in the twofold purpose of this book:

1. To serve as a supplement to a professional text by presenting selected basic concepts in the teaching of reading which can be used by a student as a preview or review of a wider discussion of the topics initiated herein.
2. To facilitate the beginning student's identification, organization, and retention of selected basic concepts in the teaching of reading by eliciting his active participation in completing the programmed lessons.*

---

*For the student who is unfamiliar with programmed instruction, it is suggested that he begin this book with Lesson Eight: Part Three — Programmed Instruction and Programmed Reading.

Acknowledgments

A special expression of appreciation is extended to Dr. Adolph Christenson, Reading Consultant, Spokane Public Schools; Dr. Vern Wade, Brigham Young University; and Dr. Douglas Burron, The University of Northern Colorado, whose perceptive criticisms of selected lessons reduced the number and the scope of errors which might have appeared in this book. Any errors which may remain are the sole responsibility of the authors.

If this book accomplishes its purposes, its success can be attributed in no small part to the candid evaluations and helpful suggestions of the many classes of undergraduate and graduate students at the University of Northern Colorado who participated in the field-testing of the lessons included herein. The authors are grateful for both their participation in the testing of the lessons and for their honesty in expressing their evaluations.

Arnold Burron

Amos L. Claybaugh

How to Use
This Book

The following suggestions may be of help to you in working through the lessons in this book:

1. Cover the answers in the column on the left with the mask provided on the inside of the back cover. After you complete an item, check your answer immediately.

2. If you find that you have provided a synonym in place of the exact response suggested in the answer column, count your answer as a correct answer.

3. A limited number of "wrong" answers is inevitable. If your response is not the same as the response provided in the answer column or if it does not express an idea similar to the idea suggested by the response provided in the answer column, it is usually desirable to go back and review a few frames.

4. The field-testing of the lessons in this book revealed that retention of the concepts presented was greater when students completed only one or two lessons during any one sitting than when the students attempted to work through a great number of lessons at one time. The questions which follow each chapter may be of assistance to you in deciding upon how much material you can comfortably cover during any one time period.

Contents

INTRODUCTION

Developing a Definition of Reading

OBJECTIVE: The reader will be able to name the two major elements usually included in a definition of reading.

definition

1. The instructional program in reading that a teacher provides for a student usually reflects the definition the teacher, himself, has for the reading process. A definition of reading should consider the translating of printed material to speech, the understanding of that printed material, and the evaluation of that material. The following frames in this lesson will attempt to aid you in formulating your own _____ of the reading process.

decoding

2. One recognized element of the reading process is the translation of the printed word back into speech. This is commonly called the *act of decoding,* for printed material can be thought of as speech written down. The act of translating printed material back into speech is called

_____.

word

decode or translate

3. The act of decoding requires that a person have control of a number of special skills called *word attack skills.* Efficient use of _____ attack skills will enable a person to successfully _____ printed material back into speech.

4. It is not enough, in any reading that a person does, to just decode the printed word back into speech successfully. Another element of the reading act is to make meaning out of what is printed; that is, to *comprehend* the material. Comprehension of what is read is another important

element

_____ of the reading act.

5. The term _comprehension_ is used too often to cover all aspects of the reading act beyond that of decoding. To do this tends to oversimplify the definition a person eventually develops for the reading process. Succeeding frames will attempt

comprehension

to further clarify the term _____.

6. One level of comprehension in reading is the _literal level_. At this level a reader is able to comprehend the obvious and direct meaning of a word, a phrase, or a sentence presented by a writer. Because of his specific purpose for reading the material, a person may only need to com-

literal

prehend what he reads at the _____ level of comprehension.

7. At times the purpose for reading a given selection requires the reader to gain an understanding that is not obviously and directly stated in the selection. To achieve his purpose, a reader must use skills called _interpretive reading skills_. Effi-

interpretive

cient and effective use of _____ reading skills will enable the person to gain the required understanding of a selection even though the meaning is not directly presented in the selection.

8. To be complete, a definition of the reading process must consider the highest level of mental activity that may be required of a person when reading for a specific purpose. This is _critical reading_, a kind of reading that requires a reader not only to _decode_ successfully, to _observe_ what is directly presented, and to _interpret_ what is not directly presented in a passage, but to do much more as well. In addition, he must _evaluate_ and _judge_ what is presented. The highest level of mental activity that may be required of a reader — evaluation and judgment — is that of

critical

_____ reading.

9. To read critically, a reader must be equipped with skills that enable him to evaluate, to challenge, to decide upon the truthfulness, the bias, and the authenticity of what is presented in print.

Critical

_____ reading requires that the reader react personally as he agrees or disagrees with the writer on the basis of his own experience, facts he has researched, or the result of his own clear-cut reasoning.

10. A program of instruction in reading, to be effective for children, would include the important elements that are incorporated into the reading

definition

process. The _____ of reading that a teacher develops for himself should be reflected in the instructional program he provides for children.

11. In this book, a number of basic concepts in the teaching of reading will be presented. As you work through the various lessons, the concepts you acquire should be of help to you in develop-

definition

ing your own _____ of reading and in establishing an instructional program which will

definition

reflect your _____ of reading.

Review Questions

1. Two major elements which are included in the process of reading are usually identified when the attempt is made to define reading. Identify these two elements. (See Frames 2 and 4 to check your answer.)

2. Several levels of reading comprehension were identified on the preceding pages. List as many of these levels as you can. (See Frames 6, 7, and 8 to check your answer.)

Significant Elements in the Reading Process

OBJECTIVE: The reader will be able to list and describe each of the reading skills known as "Word Attack Skills."

PART ONE: Word Attack Skills

1. Children who are first entering school and who have experienced the use of the English language in their homes during the preschool years normally have built up an extensive vocabulary through their listening and speaking activities. The vocabularies of such children have been estimated to be as large as 10,000 words. Vocabularies of children at the time they first enter school have developed chiefly through listen-

speaking

ing and _____ activities.

2. Words in the language can be described as having three forms: a pronunciation form, a meaning form, and a printed form. The words that make up the listening and speaking vocabularies of children when they first enter school are quite familiar to the children in their pronunciation form, are familiar in a limited way in their meaning form, and are likely to not be known in their

printed

_____ form.

3. Because the words a child has in his listening and speaking vocabularies are likely to be familiar to him only in their pronunciation and meaning forms, they must also become known to the

printed

child in their _____ forms if he is eventually to read these words. A word must be familiar to a person in its pronunciation form, its meaning form, and its printed form if it is to be

read

_____ by that person.

4. Skills that enable a person to "identify" — that is, decode — a word when it is presented in its printed form are commonly referred to as *word attack skills*. In order to pronounce a word that a person meets in its printed form, the person must

skills

decode

printed

use word attack _____. Word attack skills enable a person to identify with, or _____, a word when he meets it in its_____ form.

5. One word attack skill that a child is taught to use in attacking strange printed words is that of *context*. Context is the familiar spoken or printed material that accompanies the strange printed word. Context helps a person to choose a word that makes sense in what he is reading, but it is not used as the only word attack skill. The material that accompanies the strange word that a child is attempting to identify in printed mate-

context

rial is called _____.

6. For example, suppose a child encounters a sentence which says, "The boy rode on his horse." Suppose, further, that the child has not seen the word "horse" in print previously. In this case, given a choice between the word "horse" and, say, the word "house" as the final word in the sentence, the child would be aided in selecting the appropriate word by using the words, "The boy rode on his . . ." These words, which help the child to determine what word would make sense

context

in the sentence, constitute the _____ for the strange printed word.

7. Another word attack skill is *phonic analysis*. Phonic analysis is a skill that enables a child to use his knowledge of the sounds that letters and combinations of letters stand for in words of the English language. Letters and combinations of

sounds

letters stand for _____ in the words of a language. When a child uses his knowledge of the sounds that letters and combinations of letters stand for in words, he is using the word

phonic

analysis.

attack skill of ⎯⎯⎯⎯⎯⎯ analysis.

8. To help him in selecting a word that makes sense in relation to what he is reading, a person will

context

use ⎯⎯⎯⎯⎯⎯. To help him in identifying the actual word when he knows the sounds the letters stand for in words, a person will use his

analysis

phonic ⎯⎯⎯⎯⎯⎯ skills.

9. As words a child meets in print become more complex structurally, he will use another word attack skill called *structural analysis.* This skill will enable him to recognize common elements in words, such as root words, prefixes, suffixes, and common syllables with which he has associated sounds. When a child recognizes a familiar element in a word which he can successfully pronounce, he can be said to be using the word

structural

attack skill of ⎯⎯⎯⎯⎯⎯ analysis.

10. For words that a person has in his listening and speaking vocabularies, the use of context, phonic analysis, and structural analysis will enable him

identify or read

to ⎯⎯⎯⎯⎯⎯ these same words in print. These skills are the basic and most common

word attack

⎯⎯⎯⎯⎯⎯ ⎯⎯⎯⎯⎯⎯ skills.

11. However, a word a person meets in print may not be familiar to him in his listening and speaking vocabularies. To successfully identify this word independently, the person must use a resource beyond the common word attack skills,

context,
phonic analysis,
structural analysis

because the word attack skills of ⎯⎯⎯⎯⎯⎯,

⎯⎯⎯⎯⎯⎯ ⎯⎯⎯⎯⎯⎯ and ⎯⎯⎯⎯⎯⎯ ⎯⎯⎯⎯⎯⎯ will not be of sufficient aid.

12. A more advanced independent word attack skill used by a person to identify a strange printed word is the *use of the dictionary;* this skill can help a person establish the pronunciation and meaning of a word that is strange to him in its

printed

⎯⎯⎯⎯⎯⎯ form as well as in its spoken form.

dictionary

13. Because the word a person meets in print may be unfamiliar to him in all its forms, he needs to identify the word by skillfully using the

_____.

context

phonic analysis, struc-
tural
analysis

14. A person should use word attack skills to the extent, and only to the extent, that is required of him when he meets an unfamiliar word in print. For a word that is unfamiliar to him only

in print, the word attack skills of _____,

_____ _____, and _____

_____ will be sufficient.

dictionary

15. When a person meets a word in print that cannot be fully identified through the use of context, phonic analysis, and structural analysis, he should identify the word through the use of the

_____.

vocabularies

16. The ability to use word attack skills independently will enable a person to become familiar with words in print even though they are not presently in his listening and speaking

_____.

Review Questions

1. List three word attack skills which might be used to help a child identify a word which is strange to him in only its printed form. (See Frame 14 to check your answer.)

2. Which word attack skill should a child use to help him identify a word which is strange to him not only in its printed form, but also in its spoken form? (See Frame 12 to check your answer.)

PART TWO: Reading Comprehension

OBJECTIVE: The reader will be able to name and describe the levels of reading comprehension, as well as the subskills grouped under the heading "Critical Reading."

Levels of Comprehension

read

comprehends

comprehension

literal

inference

literal

1. The final goal of a reader is more than just translating printed material into speech. Rather, it is to react adequately to the material being

    _____.

2. *Comprehension* is a term often used to indicate that understanding of what is being read is taking place. When a reader understands what he

    is reading, it can be said that he _____ what he is reading.

3. Several levels of comprehension have been designated by reading authorities. The purpose for reading a given selection should determine the

    level of _____ a reader should attain.

4. The lowest level of comprehension enables the reader to understand the *literal* meaning of a printed passage. When a person reads and understands the message, "For protection against robbery, leave a light on in your house," he can

    be said to have comprehended the _____ meaning of the printed passage.

5. Another, and higher, level of comprehension requires the reader to *draw inference* for meaning from printed material in which the literal meaning is not directly stated. For example, a person reads, "Extreme weather conditions often adversely affect the crops in Illinois. Excessive rainfall is common in this area." To understand that too much rainfall often damages the crops in Illinois is to comprehend by means of drawing

    _____.

6. When a person understands a message that is *stated directly* in printed material, he is comprehending at the _____ level.

7. When a person understands a message in material where the meaning is only *inferred*, he is

inference

comprehending at the inferential level, indicating that he is able to draw ＿＿＿＿＿＿＿.

8. The highest level of comprehension requires the reader to evaluate and judge what is being read. Such reading is called *critical reading*. When, in addition to understanding what is stated directly and what can be only inferred, a person *evaluates* and *judges* the message on the basis of his own experience and research, he is said to be

critical

doing ＿＿＿＿＿＿ reading.

9. The way a person might read and respond to the following poster illustrates the application of the three levels of comprehension:

VOTE FOR HENRY A. SMUTHERS
(Service with Honesty)

If the person reads this poster and understands that he is being directed to vote for Henry A. Smuthers, it can be said that he has comprehended the message at the lowest level of com-

literal

prehension, referred to as the ＿＿＿＿＿＿ level.

10. In addition, if the person senses that Henry A. Smuthers is an honest man and will serve well if elected, it can be said that he comprehends the message at a higher level. He has comprehended

inferential

the message at the ＿＿＿＿＿＿ level.

11. However, if the person evaluates the message in this way, "Before I decide whether to vote for Henry A. Smuthers, I must find out more about him to determine if, to date, he has served the public honestly," it can be said that the reader has applied an even higher level of comprehension to the printed message. This higher level of comprehension requires the ability to

critical

do ＿＿＿＿＿＿ reading.

12. In reading the printed message on the poster: "Vote for Henry A. Smuthers—Service with Honesty," the reader comprehended the message on three levels:

literal

inferential

critical

the _____ level,

the _____ level,

and the level of _____ reading.

Skills for Overcoming Barriers to Comprehension

13. There are many barriers and tempting pitfalls to literal comprehension and to the eventual critical reading of printed material. The following frames will attempt to point out several of these to you. A reader must become proficient in breaking down these barriers and in avoiding these pit-

comprehend or
understand

falls in order to fully _____ what he reads.

14. One way to overcome barriers to adequate understanding of what is read is for the reader to use information present in the material itself as well as the skills he possesses. Each aid should assist the reader in achieving adequate

comprehension
or understanding

_____ of what is read.

15. One aid to comprehension is the *use of printed context*. The familiar printed material that comes before and/or after the unfamiliar word or

context

phrase is called printed _____.

16. For example, a child reads, "Fishing was bad this morning, but this afternoon I put a *Krunchette* on my line. Boy! Did I catch fish!" The word *Krunchette* is unfamiliar to the child, but he arrives at an adequate meaning for the word by

context

using the printed _____ that surrounds the word in what he read.

17. The use of context alone will not always enable the reader to arrive at an adequate meaning. Another aid to understanding incorporates the more advanced *use of the dictionary*. Because words often have multiple meanings, the meaning of a word that fits a particular context in which the word is used can be selected from those defini-

dictionary

tions presented in a _____.

18. The word *fast* is one that has many meanings. A reader might have to consult a dictionary to arrive at the appropriate meaning of the word *fast* in the following sentence: "As is the custom in their religion, the family will fast on Saturday." By selecting the appropriate meaning for

    dictionary

    the word *fast* in the _____, the reader can achieve adequate comprehension of the sentence.

19. In addition to the use of printed context and the dictionary, other aids to comprehension can be used. Read the following sentence: "The menu at the annual faculty picnic will consist of ham salad beans bread rolls chocolate ice cream cake and iced drinks." The *interpretation of punctuation marks* placed at appropriate spots in the sentence would enable the reader to more fully

    comprehend
    or understand

    _____ just what food would make up the picnic menu.

20. Writers often attempt to convey messages by using figurative as well as literal language. Figurative language can be a barrier to comprehension for it requires the reader to do something extra

    comprehension

    in order to achieve adequate _____ of what he is reading.

21. Figurative language is expressed in the form of figures of speech. Some figures of speech are in very common use; others are not. In order to comprehend the meaning a writer wishes to convey, the reader must interpret correctly these

    speech

    figures of _____.

22. When a reader meets figurative language in printed material, he is faced with two basic tasks: he must sense the literal situation in which the figure of speech is being used, and he must understand the figure of speech; that is, he must *interpret figurative language* and apply the characteristics of it to the literal situation in order to

    comprehend
    or understand

    _____ the literal meaning the writer wishes the reader to gain.

23. In the sentence: "The words of apology issued from his mouth in phrases as smooth as silk," the writer is attempting to convey to the reader a meaning that is not expressed in literal language. The phrase *smooth as silk* is not to be taken literally but is to be interpreted as a figure of speech; therefore, the reader must apply the

figurative
language

skill of interpreting _____ _____.

24. The sample sentence in the preceding frame described how an apology was made. Although the phrase *smooth as silk* has no literal association with the situation, the reader can apply his understanding of the phrase to the literal situation and arrive at adequate comprehension by

interpreting,
figurative language

_____ the _____ _____.

25. Although figurative language often makes for more interesting reading, it can be a barrier to gaining the meaning of what the writer wishes

comprehend
or understand

the reader to _____ even though the reader can use context and the dictionary adequately.

26. Still another barrier to comprehension is the tendency on the part of the reader to think of each sentence as a unit of meaning separate from and unrelated to other sentences in the paragraph. To build a mental fence around each sentence in a paragraph, rather than sensing the contribution that each sentence is making to the main topic of the paragraph, is to reduce the pos-

comprehend
or understand

sibility that the reader will _____ fully the meaning the writer wished to convey by the paragraph.

27. Although a paragraph often has a topic sentence which reveals the main idea, a paragraph need not have a sentence that acts as a topic sentence. It often takes several sentences of a paragraph, each making a small contribution to the

topic

_____, to reveal to the reader just what is being discussed in the paragraph.

28. Read the paragraph that follows:

> Hummingbirds are much smaller than sparrows. They like colored sugar water for food. They drink the colored water from glass-tubed feeders. They put their beaks into the tube. Hummingbirds can fly in one spot when they feed. If you're quiet, they'll drink even if you're close to the feeder.

What this paragraph is about is not revealed by just one topic sentence but by sensing the relationship among the sentences which together

topic   reveal the _____ of the paragraph.

29. The preceding example illustrates that a reader must often *sense the relationship among sentences* in a paragraph in order to determine the topic of the paragraph. This skill, as well as the previously identified skills of using printed

context, dictionary   _____, the use of the _____,

punctuation   interpreting _____, and the interpreta-

figurative   tion of _____ language, enables a reader to more adequately comprehend printed material.

30. A further barrier to comprehension is the failure of the reader to keep in mind that printed material is essentially written speech; therefore, when going over the material, the reader should think of it as speech. In doing this, he will tend to stress, or intonate, words and phrases in a way that reveals meaning. *Sensing the correct intonation* of the material being read will help the

comprehension   reader to achieve adequate _____ of the printed material.

31. The following sentence is written without internal punctuation and gives the reader no cue to intonation: "If you don't help Mary you'll be late for the parade." Read the sentence, varying the points of intonation. The intonation in the sentence determines the meaning conveyed by the sentence. Therefore, sensing the correct

intonation   _____ will help the reader to achieve adequate comprehension of the sentence.

32. One other barrier to comprehension of printed material is neglect on the part of the reader to use his ability to visualize the events being described in the printed material. The *ability to visualize* develops from the accumulation of experiences and the development of concepts from

experiences these ——————.

33. Does anything in your experience enable you to visualize the following?

It was a very hot day in midsummer. One boy was invited by his friend to come to his house where his mother had a treat for them. A few minutes later, Mrs. Benjamin placed before her son's friend a large bowl containing freshly baked shortcake almost hidden by fresh, slightly sugared strawberries and topped with chilled whipped cream. This was the "last word" in summer refreshment.

Surely the reader understood the situation more fully because, from his own experiences, he pos-

visualize sessed the ability to —————— the event.

34. The preceding frames have identified several skills used in overcoming problems of meaning that are often met in printed materials. The reader who can use one or a combination of these skills when the need arises should be able to achieve

comprehension full —————— of what he is attempting to read.

Skills at the Critical Level of Comprehension

35. To understand what is read is not necessarily to read the material critically. In addition to understanding, an evaluating and judging of what is read is essential to the process of reading

critically ——————.

36. There are many common pitfalls between comprehending what is read and *critically reading* what is read. The following frames will point out

critical a number of the pitfalls that hinder —————— reading.

37. It is not uncommon for children and even adults to assume that what is seen in print is basically true. However, it is less likely that printed material would be readily accepted as being basically

critical

true if a reader applied the skill of _____ reading to the printed material.

38. Sometimes the *use of one's own experience* is extensive enough to determine if what is read is true or not. A person, regardless of age, should be encouraged to evaluate the truth of a state-

experience(s)

ment by using his own _____ to check the truth of a statement.

39. For example, a person might read an account of an experience in a snow storm in Wisconsin. Descriptions in the account might appear ridiculously fantastic to most readers. Yet, this particular reader might be able to judge the truth of the description because such storms had been

experience

part of his own _____.

40. However, it is likely that the experience a person brings to printed material is not extensive enough to judge its truth or validity adequately. He must then be equipped to use additional procedures

truth or validity

to determine the _____ of what is being read.

41. Another useful skill in reading critically is to *distinguish statements of fact from statements of opinion* and to determine the validity of each. Valid information can be written and presented either as statements of fact or as statements of opinion. Critical reading of the information

distinguish

would require the reader to _____ statements of fact from statements of opinion.

42. How information is presented, in itself, does not determine its validity. Statements of opinion, as well as statements of fact, must be read critically

validity

to determine their _____.

43. How information is presented does not determine if it is good or bad. Information presented

bad

critically

fact, opinion

opinion

statement

validity

as an opinion may be either good or _____.

44. Regardless of whether a bit of information is presented as fact or opinion, the reader must determine the validity of the information presented by reading the information _____.

45. The preceding frames indicate that critical reading involves *determining the validity of information,* as well as the ability to distinguish _____ from _____.

46. Consider the following statement: "As I see it, the decision to permit a business to be established at the corner of Lombard Avenue and Third Street was a poor one. Local residences will certainly depreciate in value as they suffer from the invasion of retail activities." Words and phrases in this statement lead a person to sense that it is not a statement of fact, but is a statement of _____.

47. In reading the above statement critically, the reader must decide whether supporting evidence is available if he is to determine the validity of the _____.

48. In referring to the statement in frame 46, a critical reader would likely investigate who it was that made the statement. His research might well reveal that the statement was made by a person whose profession is the planning and modification of urban areas. This fact will help the reader to determine the _____ of the statement of opinion in frame 46.

49. In addition to the applying of his experience, the distinguishing of statements of fact from those of opinion, and the determining of the validity of printed material, a reader must be able to *identify propaganda* which might be present in a printed statement. Propaganda is written material that attempts to persuade the reader to think or act in a given way. Like statements of opinion, statements containing propaganda material are

propaganda

not necessarily good or bad. It is the reader's task to recognize the presence of _____ in a statement and consider its validity.

50. A newspaper advertisement might present this statement: "Joe Smith, the brightest star in contemporary golf competition, dusts his feet with Walk-Ease Foot Powder before each round of play." To persuade readers to use this product,

propaganda

a _____ technique is used in this advertisement.

51. It is essential that the reader learn to identify

propaganda

_____ in a statement and check further to determine its validity if he is to read the

critically

statement _____.

52. Many abilities are required of the reader if he is to avoid the pitfalls which might stand in the way of fully comprehending a given statement. To understand the content of the statement often is not sufficient. The reader must read the statement critically by applying his experience and the

fact

skills of distinguishing _____ from

opinion, validity

_____, determining the _____

propaganda

of the statement, and identifying _____ which might be present in the statement.

53. The reader must possess certain abilities in order to overcome common barriers to understanding and to avoid pitfalls which might lead him to draw false conclusions. Such abilities will enable the person to attack printed material as a critical

reader

_____.

Review Questions

1. Several levels of comprehension have been identified in this lesson. Identify each of the levels presented. (See Frame 12 to check your answer.)

2. Several skills have been identified for overcoming barriers to com-

prehension. List as many of these skills as you can. (See Frames 29 through 34 to check your answer.)

3. Several skills which can be used in avoiding pitfalls to critical reading have been identified in this lesson. List as many of these skills as you can. (See Frame 52 to check your answer.)

PART THREE: Reading Study Skills

OBJECTIVE: The reader will be able to name and describe the reading study skills and provide an example of how each skill might be used by a student in pursuing information through reading.

1. As a person learns to read, he will find more and more opportunities to use his reading ability to further his learning. The *reading study skills* will enable him to learn efficiently and effectively from printed material. Skills that assist a person to learn efficiently and effectively when using printed materials are called reading study

skills

_____.

2. For example, a student has accepted a social studies assignment which he will research through printed materials. He is to find the importance that the long rifle played in the life of the early pioneers of our country. The assignment calls for the student to make an oral report two weeks hence. To prepare an effective report from printed materials, the student will be ex-

reading

pected to use efficiently the _____

study

_____ skills.

3. Initially, to become acquainted with the common reading study skills, let's consider what the student above has to do to accomplish his social

assignment

studies _____.

4. The student's first task is to locate information he may be able to use in his report. To do so efficiently, he must use a major reading study skill, that of *location*. Procedures and activities that make up the skill that enables a person to

location

find information in printed materials constitute the skill of _____.

5. However, all information located that is related to an assignment may not be usable or valid in that assignment. The information must be evaluated to determine if it is usable and_____ for the assignment.

valid

6. Besides the skill of location a student would have to use a second major reading study skill, that of *evaluation*. To determine whether certain information is usable and valid in fulfilling an assignment, the student must use the reading study skill of _____.

evaluation

7. For example, suppose that a student, in looking for information about the long rifle, locates an authoritative reference work on pistols. In deciding that this reference work is not a source which would be usable and valid for his assignment, the student would be using the reading study skill of _____.

evaluation

8. To find information related to an assignment in an efficient way, a person is required to use the reading study skill of _____.

location

9. In order to determine whether related information is usable and valid in an assignment, a person is required to use the reading study skill of _____.

evaluation

10. At this point, the student has located information that is both usable and valid in fulfilling his assignment. He must now organize the information so he can use it in making his report. A third reading study skill is that of *organization*. Putting collected information in a form suitable for fulfilling an assignment requires a person to employ this third major reading study skill, that of _____.

organization

11. If the student reads his report verbatim, it often lacks the dynamics necessary to hold the listener's interest and attention. In order to keep constant eye contact with his audience, the student giving an oral report will need, for the most part, to retain in his mind the information he desires to report. *Retention* is a fourth major reading

skill

    study _____.

12. The procedures and aids that a person uses to assist himself in retaining the usable and valid information organized for an oral report consti-

retention

    tute the major reading study skill of_____.

13. As the reader locates various materials and attempts to evaluate and organize information, he will probably not read each source with the same intensity. Some material may require a slow rate of reading, while other material may be read at a

rate

    faster rate. *Using an appropriate* _____ of reading is a fifth major study skill.

14. Frequently, information required to complete a study skill assignment is presented graphically, in the form of a diagram, a chart, a map, or another graphic aid. The *ability to read graphic aids* is a

study skill

    sixth major _____ _____.

15. Situations that require a person to use printed material to gain the information needed to extend his learning make it essential for him to use

location

evaluation

organization

retention

    the reading study skills of _____ of information, _____ of the usefulness and validity of information, _____ of information to be used, and _____ of information. In addition, the possessor of efficient reading study skills will use an appropriate

rate

    _____ of reading in his studying, and he will be able to interpret maps, charts, dia-

graphic aids

    grams, or other _____ _____.

reading study

skills

16. The six skills mentioned in the preceding frames are referred to as the _____ _____

_____.

Review Question

Six skills are required by the reader in preparing an assignment involving printed material. Name these skills. (See Frame 15 to check your answer.)

Readiness
for Reading

OBJECTIVE: Upon completion of parts One and Two, the reader will be able to state how each of the reading readiness factors might be related to learning to read.

PART ONE: Factors Contributing to Readiness for Reading

In the situation described below, a father of six sons called his sons together to give them directions in completing a task. The father informed his sons that the task was very important. He also acknowledged the possibility that several of his sons might experience failure by telling his sons that he would send them out one at a time until one of the sons had completed the task successfully. Even though the task was not unduly difficult and even though the father's directions were very clear, each son, in turn, failed to complete the task. The father's directions and the sons' experiences follow. When you have finished reading the description below, try to identify the reasons why each son failed. Then complete the frames on the following pages to determine whether the reasons you have chosen are similar to those presented in the frames. The portion of the chapter which follows the introductory frames will help you to build an understanding of the concept of *readiness*.

The father's directions:

"Travel the trail through the mountains which leads to four roads. When you reach the four roads, follow the north road. Remain on this road until you reach a stand of aspen trees. Turn in the direction of the aspen trees and continue in this direction until you reach some signs. Read the signs and follow the sign which directs you to the easiest route down the mountainside. Proceed down and then climb the steep ridge which will be opposite you. On the other side of the ridge you will find what you need to complete the task which I have assigned to you."

The sons' experiences:

Immediately after hearing the instructions, the first son, who had been raised by relatives in a foreign country and who did not have a full command of the English language, departed. After traveling only a short way, however, he turned back. While thinking over what his father had said, he had discovered that because of his unfamiliarity with the English language, he had not understood the directions completely.

The second son then departed. He soon reached the four roads his father had described. He then took the fourth road, which led south. In listening to his father's directions, he had heard the word as "fourth" when his father had said "north." When he failed to return, the third son departed.

On reaching the four roads, the third son followed the north road. He soon reached the stand of aspen trees but was puzzled by a stand of poplar trees which stood opposite the aspen trees. Although he had identified aspen trees in the past, he now could not tell which of the two stands of similar trees was the stand of aspen trees. After careful deliberation, he turned in the direction of the poplar trees and soon lost his way. When the third son also failed to return, the fourth son departed.

Proceeding quickly, the fourth son reached the four roads, followed the north road, turned in the direction of the stand of aspens, and reached the signs his father had described. The signs, however, were international trail signs, indicating the relative difficulty of various ski trails. Since the fourth son had had no previous experience in reading trail signs, he despondently returned home.

When the fourth son arrived home, the fifth son departed. The fifth son found all of the directions easy to follow, read the trail signs, and continued on his journey. By this time, however, he had lost interest in the task. But since he had only his father's word that the task was very important, he soon became lost in conversation and companionship with a group of young skiers who happened to be passing by.

When it became obvious that the fifth son had failed, the sixth son departed. The sixth son took the north road, turned in the direction of the aspen trees, followed the correct sign downhill, passed his errant brother, and began his struggle up the steep ridge. Despite strenuous effort, however, he lacked the physical endurance to complete the climb. After recovering part of his strength, he slowly trudged homeward to tell his father the disappointing news that all six sons had failed.

——————————————————————————List the reasons why each son failed:

1. _____

2. _____

3. _____

4. _____

5. _____

6. _____

PART TWO: Reading Readiness Factors

language

failure

fourth

failure

see

experience

interest

task

experience

1. The first son experienced failure in his attempt to complete the task because he could not understand all of his father's directions since he was not familiar with the English _____.

2. Unless the first son acquired familiarity with the English language, he would probably again experience _____ in other tasks requiring familiarity with the English language.

3. The second son experienced failure because he could not hear the difference between the word "north" and the word "_____."

4. In other tasks requiring the same ability to hear slight differences in the sounds of words, the second son would probably again experience _____.

5. The third son experienced failure because he could not see the slight difference between similar objects. It is probable that the third son would again experience failure in other tasks requiring the ability to _____ slight differences between similar objects.

6. Of the remaining three sons, the fourth son failed because he had no previous _____ in reading trail signs. The fifth son experienced failure because he had no _____ in completing the task, since he had only his father's opinion that the task was important; the sixth son failed because he lacked the physical endurance to complete the _____.

7. The fourth son probably would fail at other tasks requiring previous _____ in reading trail signs; the fifth son probably would

interest

endurance

different

task

abilities

physical strength

physical strength

readiness

fail at other tasks in which he had no

_____; and the sixth son probably
would fail at other tasks requiring physical

_____.

8. Although each young man failed to complete the task, it can be seen that each one failed for a different reason. The reason for failure was different for each son, but the task itself was not

_____ for each son.

9. The reason for each son's failure cannot be found in the task itself; however, the reason for failure can be found by identifying the particular abilities with which each son approached the

_____.

10. If successful completion of a task required six different abilities, a person possessing only three or four abilities probably would fail to complete the task successfully. The task could be completed successfully, however, by a person who

possessed the six different _____ required by the task.

11. It can be seen, then, that the difficulty of any given task for any given individual depends, in part, on the abilities with which the individual approaches the task. For example, if a task requires physical strength, a desirable quality to possess in undertaking the task would be

_____ _____.

12. In the case of an individual endowed with physical strength, a task requiring only physical strength would not be difficult for him because he is ready for the task. The factor which would make the individual ready for the task — the *readiness factor* — would be the factor of

_____ _____.

13. In tasks requiring physical strength, the quality of physical strength is a _____ factor which is related to probable success in completing the tasks.

14. Human beings have an abundance of qualities which enable them to be ready to undertake a variety of tasks. The particular qualities which can be applied to the undertaking of any task, however, are determined by the nature of the

task
_____.

15. Hence, if success in a task depended only upon an individual's prior experience with a similar task, and not upon his physical strength, the quality of physical strength would not be a readiness factor related to the task. In this case, the readi-

prior

experience
ness factor would be the factor of _____

_____.

16. Even though a person might possess physical strength, then, the quality of physical strength probably would not contribute to a person's success in undertaking a task requiring only prior

experience
_____.

17. Physical strength, in this case, would not need to be applied, because it is not a readiness factor. Prior experience, on the other hand, could

readiness

factor
be applied, because it is a _____

_____.

18. If a person's probable success in undertaking a given task would be enhanced in the event that the person possessed both physical strength *and* prior experience with a similar task, physical strength and prior experience would then both

readiness factors
be _____ _____.

19. Readiness factors are any qualities, abilities, or experiences which can contribute in some way to the achieving of success in a particular

task
_____.

20. The nature of a task determines which specific factors, among a variety of factors, can be identi-

readiness
fied as _____ factors.

21. The task of learning to ice skate, for example, is of a different nature than the task of learning how to read. Since the tasks are different, the readi-

different

ness factors which may contribute to probable success in undertaking each task may also be _____.

task

22. It is possible for an individual to possess a large number of desirable qualities, abilities, or experiences and still fail to be ready to undertake a particular _____.

read

23. For example, a person who is undertaking the task of learning to read could possess desirable qualities, such as physical attractiveness, a pleasant disposition, and well-developed physical strength. However, although these factors might contribute to the person's probable success in a variety of tasks, they would not necessarily contribute to his success in undertaking the task of learning to _____.

readiness

24. To determine which specific qualities might be readiness factors which could contribute to a child's probable success in learning to read, the task of learning to read can be studied, since the nature of a task determines which specific factors, among a variety of factors, can be identified as _____ factors.

words or
material

25. In identifying the elements comprising the reading task, an earlier chapter pointed out that reading requires the acts of decoding and comprehending printed _____.

form

26. To decode and to comprehend a word in its printed form — that is, to *read* the word — it is necessary that the learner be familiar with the word in its spoken or oral _____. It is also desirable that the learner be familiar with the words constituting the context for the strange printed

word

_____.

context

27. For example, if a child had never heard the word "beautician," it would not be likely that he could decode this word even though he might be familiar with most of the other words which constitute the printed _____ for the strange printed word.

28. If a child had previously heard the word "beautician," however, and if he encountered this word in the context of a sentence such as, "Mother had her hair done by a beautician," it is probable that the child could use the context, other word attack skills, and his familiarity with oral language to decode the word which is strange to him only

form

in its printed ——————.

29. Since it is likely that a child with good word attack skills will successfully decode and comprehend a word with which he is familiar in its oral form, such familiarity with words, or *oral language facility,* can be identified as a reading

readiness

—————— factor.

30. The fact that oral language facility can be identified as a reading readiness factor means, simply, that ability in the use of language that a child is learning to read probably will contribute to the child's success in undertaking the task of learn-

read

ing to ——————.

31. Although oral language facility is an important reading readiness factor, it is not a *guarantee* that a child will fully comprehend an idea even though the words used to express the idea are strange to the child only in their printed

form

——————.

32. For example, a child raised on a ranch would be less likely to fully comprehend a story about life in a large city than a child raised in the

city

——————.

33. A child raised in a city, reading a story about life in a city, would likely have a broad background of experiences in city life. These experiences would probably help him to understand the story. A child raised on a ranch would probably not reach an equal depth of understanding in reading about city life, because he would not

background

be likely to have a broad —————— of experiences in city life.

34. A child raised on a ranch would probably understand more fully a story about problems of life

on a ranch, however, because of his broad

**background,
experiences**

_____ of _____ in ranch life.

35. A child's depth of understanding in reading about an experience that someone else might have had is affected by the extent of his real or vicarious

experience

participation in a similar _____.

36. Since a broad background of experience probably will contribute to a child's success in undertaking the task of learning to read, _experiential background_ can be identified as a reading

readiness

_____ factor.

37. Oral language facility and a broad background of experiences, although desirable reading readiness qualities, are of limited value to a child in learning to distingush letter forms and the sounds they represent. A knowledge of the sounds letters represent is important to use in conjunction with context clues which, when used alone, usually will not enable a child to identify a word which

form

is strange to him in its printed _____.

38. In order to learn letter forms and the sounds they represent, a child must be able to hear differences in letter sounds and to see differences in letter

forms

_____.

39. For example, a child would have a difficult time in learning the sound which the letter _b_ represents in the word "big," and the sound which the letter _d_ represents in the word "dig," unless

hear

he could first _____ the difference between the word "big" and the word "dig."

40. Suppose, though, that a child _could_ discriminate between the sounds of the words "big" and "dig." He still may not be able to recognize the sounds represented by the letters _d_ and _b_ unless

**forms or
   shapes**

he could see the difference in the _____
of the letters _d_ and _b_.

41. The ability to _hear_ differences among similar-sounding letters is sometimes called _auditory_

discrimination. The ability to *see* differences among letters of similar form is sometimes called

discrimination

visual _____.

42. Since the contrast in the sounds of many words and many letters is minimal and since the contrast in the appearance of many words and many letters is minimal, the skill of auditory discrimination and the skill of visual discrimination would need to be applied in learning to read. These skills, then, can be identified as reading

readiness

_____ factors.

43. The fact that auditory discrimination and visual discrimination can be identified as reading readiness factors means, simply, that the ability to

sounds

hear differences among letter _____ and the ability to see differences among letter

forms

_____ will probably contribute to a child's success in undertaking the task of learning to read.

44. Abilities in visual discrimination and in auditory discrimination, however, do not *guarantee* that a child will not experience difficulties in learning to read. Even though a child can hear and see the difference in the sounds and forms of the letters *d* and *b,* for example, he might lack the intelligence to associate the appropriate sound

letter or symbol
or form

with the appropriate _____.

45. A child of below normal intelligence might also lack the ability to identify, for example, the main idea of a story or to recall what he has read. These limitations would detract from his

comprehension or
understanding

_____ of what he is trying to read.

46. Although children of low intelligence can be taught to read, it is probable that children who are not limited by low intelligence will have less difficulty in learning to read than children who are limited by low intelligence. *Intelligence,* then,

reading

can be identified as still another _____

readiness

_____ factor.

47. Suppose, though, that a child of normal or above normal intelligence has a negative attitude toward reading or a lack of interest in learning how to read. His negative attitude and lack of interest likely will prevent him from applying his normal

    intelligence   or above normal _____ to the task of learning how to read.

48. A child's negative attitude toward reading or his lack of interest in learning how to read also may prevent him from applying other desirable read-

    readiness   ing _____ factors to the task of learning

    read   how to _____.

49. Since a negative attitude or a lack of interest might detract from a child's probable success in undertaking the task of learning to read, the child who possesses these undesirable qualities will

    ready   probably not be _____ to undertake the task of learning to read.

50. On the other hand, if a child possesses a positive attitude and high interest, the presence of these desirable qualities will be a partial indication that

    ready   the child is probably _____ to read.

51. The factors of attitude and interest can influence negatively or positively the probable degree of success a child will experience in undertaking the task of learning to read. *Attitude* and *interest,*

    readiness   then, can be identified as reading _____ factors.

52. Application of a positive attitude and high interest, as well as other desirable reading readiness factors, usually takes place within a learning group in a classroom. Successful participation in classroom groups requires emotional and social maturity on the part of the child. The ability to cooperate with a teacher and with group members is evidence of emotional and social

    maturity   _____.

53. The ability to accept direction and guidance from a teacher and the ability to work independently

emotional

social maturity

also are evidence of a child's _____ and

_____ _____.

54. The ability to listen quietly to a lesson in, say, auditory discrimination would be further evi-

emotional, social

dence of a child's _____ and _____ maturity.

55. Suppose, though, that a child lacks desirable emotional and social qualities which would en-able him to learn effectively in a typical class-room group learning situation. If he refuses, for example, to listen quietly to a lesson in auditory discrimination, he cannot be expected to de-velop the ability to distinguish differences in

sounds

letter _____.

56. A child who lacks emotional and social maturity probably will not learn effectively in most other classroom situations. Behaviors, such as with-drawal, aggression, extreme shyness, or inability to work independently, will keep him from apply-ing his intelligence, experience, or other

reading readiness

_____ _____ factors to the task of learning how to read.

57. On the other hand, a child who possesses qual-

emotional, social

ities of _____ and _____ ma-turity required for classroom group learning experiences probably will be able to apply desir-able reading readiness factors to the task of learn-ing how to read.

58. The presence of the qualities of emotional and social maturity will be a partial indication that

ready

a child is _____ to work in a classroom group situation.

59. Since the task of learning to read is usually under-taken in a classroom group learning situation and since emotional and social maturity are factors which contribute to a child's readiness for a class-room group learning situation, *emotional* and *social maturity* can be identified as reading

readiness

_____ factors.

guarantee

60. Earlier in this chapter, it was pointed out that the presence of any given reading readiness factor does not *guarantee* that a child will experience success in learning how to read. Similarly, emotional and social maturity, although they are desirable readiness factors, do not _____ that a child will probably experience success in learning to read.

readiness factors

61. Since no single reading readiness factor is a guarantee that a child will experience success in learning to read, it can be concluded that readiness for reading is indicated by the presence of a combination of reading _____ _____.

language

62. For example, successful decoding and comprehension of words which are strange in their printed form are enhanced by the presence of the reading readiness factor of oral _____ facility.

background

experiences

63. For full understanding of an idea, however, a child needs not only the quality of oral language facility, but he also needs a broad _____ of _____.

discrimination

visual

64. Oral language facility and a broad background of experiences are not the only reading readiness factors desirable for learning letter sounds and letter forms. For success in distinguishing among letter sounds and letter forms, a child must possess the ability to apply the reading readiness factors of auditory _____ and _____ discrimination.

intelligence

65. To avoid undue difficulty in associating a letter with the sound it represents or to avoid difficulty in comprehension, a child should possess the reading readiness quality of normal _____.

facility

66. To apply the reading readiness factors of oral language _____, a broad background of

experiences, discrimination	——————————, visual ——————————, auditory
discrimination, intelligence	——————————, and normal ——————————, a
attitude	child would need to have a positive ——————————
interest	toward reading, and a high —————————— in learning how to read.

67. Finally, since all of the reading readiness factors usually are required for learning which takes place within a classroom group situation, a child should possess qualities of emotional and social

maturity   —————————— in order to learn effectively as a member of a classroom group.

PART THREE: Assessing Readiness for Reading

OBJECTIVE: The reader will be able to describe techniques for assessing readiness for reading.

1. Since the successful undertaking of a task is not likely to occur unless an individual is ready for the task, the teacher, before assigning a task, will probably want to determine whether a child is

ready   —————————— for the task.

2. Early success in a task, rather than failure, is desirable. Therefore, if it is possible to assess the extent to which an individual might possess qualities which could be applied to a task — that is, to assess his readiness for the task — it is desirable that an attempt be made to assess the

readiness   individual's —————————— for the task before assigning the task.

3. Suppose, for example, that a father was preparing to assign to one of his sons a task requiring only physical endurance. If a father wanted to have an idea of each son's readiness for the task, he could try to determine which sons have the

physical endurance   quality of —————————— ——————————.

4. One way for the father to determine which of his sons would be most likely to succeed at the task

requiring physical endurance would be for him to observe his sons to find evidence of

physical endurance

_____ _____.

5. The father could also consult with others who had observed his sons or with the sons them- selves in order to obtain information about each

physical endurance

son's _____ _____.

6. For example, one son in the narrative at the be- ginning of this lesson had been raised by rela- tives. To obtain information about the son's physical endurance, the father would probably

relatives or people

want to consult with the _____ who had raised this son or with the son himself.

7. Suppose, however, that a father wanted to deter- mine his sons' abilities before assigning them a task which required abilities not easily observ- able. For a task requiring, say, visual discrimina- tion, the father might evaluate each son's ability by constructing a similar task requiring the ability

visual discrimination

of _____ _____.

8. In situations in which information about a spe- cific ability could not be attained readily through observation or consultation with others, the father probably would test his sons by assigning

task

a task similar to the _____ to be per- formed at a future time.

9. It can be seen, then, that if the presence or ab- sence of a desired quality could be identified through *observation,* the father probably would try to make a decision on the basis of

observation

_____.

10. Similarly, if the presence or absence of a desired quality could be identified through *consultation with others* or with the son himself, the father probably would try to make a decision on the

consultation

basis of _____ with others.

11. If the presence or absence of a desired quality could be identified on the basis of a *test of per-*

formance in a task requiring abilities similar to those required by a future task, the father probably would make his decision on the basis of a

test

_____ of performance.

12. If, however, the presence or absence of a desired quality could be identified on the basis of observation, consultation with others and with each son, as well as on a test of performance, the

observation

father would be wise to use _____,

consultation

_____ with others and with each son,

test

and a _____ of performance, before reaching a decision.

13. The father probably would use as many avenues as possible in finding a base for his decision regarding the presence or absence of any particular

quality or ability

_____ that his sons might possess.

14. Similarly a teacher preparing to help a child to undertake the task of learning to read, probably would use as many avenues as possible on which to base a decision regarding the extent of a child's readiness for undertaking the task of

read

learning to _____.

15. This means, then, that when the extent to which a particular quality is present in a child can be determined, in part, by observation, the teacher

observation

can use _____ to obtain information about the child's readiness for reading.

16. When the extent to which a particular quality is present can be determined, in part, by consulta-

consultation

tion, the teacher can use _____, as well as other means, in finding a base for a decision about the child's readiness for reading.

17. When observation and consultation are not sufficient indicators of the extent to which a particular quality is present, the teacher can use a

test

_____ of performance that requires abilities which are desirable in approaching the task of learning to read.

observation,
    consultation

test

18. Three methods of assessing readiness, then, which can be used singly or in combination, would be _____ of a child, _____ with the child and with others, and a _____ of performance.

19. If a test of performance is used, the test of performance would be based upon reading readiness factors. Since the objective of a test based upon reading readiness factors is the assessment of a child's readiness for reading, it is logical to assume that such a test would be called a

reading

_____ readiness test.

20. Reading readiness tests can be constructed by a teacher. Professionally prepared tests are also available. These tests can be useful to teachers who desire information which is difficult to assess

observation

through _____ of a child and through

consultation

_____ with the child or with others.

21. Just as success in reading cannot be guaranteed by the presence of any one desirable readiness quality, accurate assessment of reading readiness cannot be guaranteed on the basis of any one procedure. A thorough assessment of a child's readiness for reading would involve assessment

observation

through _____ of a child, assessment

consultation

through _____ with the child and with others, and assessment through the use of

reading

_____ readiness tests.

Review Questions

1. How would you define the term "readiness factor"? (See Frame 19 in Part One of this chapter to check your answer.)

2. List the reading readiness factors presented in Part One of this chapter. (See Frames 66 and 67 of Part One to check your answer.)

3. Identify three ways in which readiness for reading can be assessed. (See Frame 21 of Part Two to check your answer.)

Assessing Reading Ability

OBJECTIVE: Upon completion of parts One, Two, and Three, the reader will be able to:
1. describe the basic principles of assessment;
2. define the terms *standardized test, survey test, diagnostic test, raw score, grade equivalent score,* and *centile score;*
3. state the differences between informal assessment and formal assessment.

PART ONE: What Should Be Assessed — Approaches to Assessment

1. In any activity involving a deliberate attempt to achieve a predetermined goal, one important factor contributing to success in reaching the goal is the factor of assessment. If, for example, a golfer pauses in his game to consider the position of his grip on the club or to reflect upon the

assessment

path of his swing, he is including _____ in his attempts to shoot a good game of golf.

2. Although synonyms for assessment, such as *diagnosis, evaluation, measurement,* and *appraisal* can convey different nuances, or slightly different meanings, the term *assessment* in this lesson will be used as a synonym for each of the other terms. The activities implied by each of the other terms are a part of assessment, and each of the terms can be used to express the idea that some kind of

assessment

_____is taking place.

3. Returning to the example of the golfer who is seeking to improve his game, it would be logical to assume that the golfer, in his assessment activities, probably would not consider factors associated with his attempts at skiing a few weeks earlier, since the factors associated with his skiing experience would not likely be related to success

golf

in playing _____.

assessment

4. On the other hand, if the golfer had sprained his wrist while skiing and if the effects of the sprain still bothered him, he probably would include this aspect of his skiing experience in his

   _____ of factors assocated with his attempts to shoot a good game of golf.

5. In the assessment of his golf game, the golfer would *consider information* which might appear to have the possibility of being either directly or potentially related to his efforts to play a good game of golf. If the golfer decides to assess his ability in skiing, he would *consider information* which might appear to have the possibility of being either directly or potentially related to the

skiing

   sport of _____.

information

6. The activity of assessment always involves a con-

   sideration of _____ which appears to have the possibility of being either directly or potentially related to whatever is being assessed.

7. Since the activity of assessment always involves a consideration of information, one important step

information

   in assessment is the gathering of _____.

8. It is possible to employ a *variety of approaches* in gathering information for purposes of assessment. For example, a golfer might assess the appropriateness of his swing by soliciting the evaluation of the club pro, by observing himself on videotape, or by comparing his swing with the swing of another golfer with good form. The golfer would then be using a variety of

approaches

   _____ to obtain the information he desires.

9. Similarly, a teacher, in striving to achieve his goal of establishing or maintaining a desirable program of reading instruction, could use a variety

approaches

   of _____ to obtain information which would appear to have the possibility of being either directly or potentially related to his goal.

10. Suppose, for example, that a teacher wanted to determine whether students were interested in a

display of supplementary reading materials he had provided. The teacher probably would observe his students to see whether they demonstrated their interest by examining the supplementary reading _____.

materials

11. In trying to assess student interest in his display, the teacher could use *casual observation* to obtain the information he required. However, if the teacher wanted to go beyond an assessment of interest to an assessment of whether the students were actually reading the material, he probably would increase his amount of _____ to include an assessment of what the students were doing with the materials they were selecting.

observation

12. To obtain information that would help him to determine whether his students had actually read the materials, the teacher also might employ a test or assignment that would assess the students' awareness of concepts presented in the _____.

materials

13. In each case, the choice of the approach used to obtain information would be influenced, in part, by the particular factor the teacher wanted to _____ and by the extent to which he wanted to assess it.

assess

14. It might be said, then, that the *nature* of what is to be assessed and the *extent* to which it is to be assessed influence, in part, the choice of the *method* by which it will be _____.

assessed

15. Another way of stating the preceding frame is that *what* you want to know (that is, the *kind* of information you want) and *how much* you want to know will be important influences on your selection of the *method* you will use to obtain the necessary _____.

information

16. To proceed with this idea, let's say that a teacher wanted to know how well the pupils in his class had achieved in their reading abilities following a given period of instruction in comparison with

another class of similar children in the same grade. The teacher probably could have a discussion with the teacher of the other class in

achievement

order to compare the _____ of each class.

17. Suppose, though, that the teacher of the other class wanted a more objective comparison. He might suggest that the method used should involve the administering of a test to each class and that both teachers would administer the same test in the same way, allowing each class the same amount of time to complete the test. For the more objective comparison suggested by the second teacher, the teachers could compare the

test

average _____ achievement of the first

test

class with the average _____ achievement of the second class.

18. In each case, *what* the teachers wanted to know was how the achievement of one class compared with the achievement of the other class. But since the second teacher was apparently not satisfied with the *kind* of information which might be obtained in a discussion with the first

method

teacher, he suggested a different _____ of obtaining information.

19. In this situation, then, the *kind* of information the second teacher wanted influenced his choice

method

of the _____ of obtaining the information.

20. Had the second teacher wanted more information than test achievement on which to base a comparison, he might have suggested still an-

information

other method of obtaining _____ .

21. In this case, *how much* he might want to know (that is, the extent of the information he wanted) would have influenced his choice of the

method

_____ of obtaining information.

22. It is important to be aware of the fact that the *nature* of what is to be assessed and the *extent*

to which it is to be assessed are important influences in the choice of a method for assessment. Conferences on pupil achievement, for example, would not be an appropriate method to use if a teacher wanted to compare his class with a large number of classes selected from other schools and other districts, since it would not be likely that a teacher could hold

conferences

_____ with all other teachers of all other classes in all other districts.

23. Since it would not be likely that a teacher could confer with all other teachers of all other similar classes in all other districts, the teacher would have to employ some other method to

compare

_____ the achievement of his class with the achievement of a large number of other, similar classes.

24. The teacher might then decide to use a *standardized test* to obtain information for a comparison, since standardized tests are a commonly accepted method of comparing the test performance of a child or a class in relation to the performance of a large number of similar children in a representative population who had taken the same

test

_____.

25. Included in standardized tests are instructions for expressing a child's raw score — the number of items he answered correctly—in a form which is more meaningful to a teacher than is the raw score. Thus, a raw score might be expressed in the form of a grade level, an index of performance which is likely to be more meaningful for

raw

a teacher than a _____ score.

26. For example, suppose a child answered sixty-six questions correctly on the "reading" section of a standardized test. His raw score (sixty-six) would probably not be very meaningful to his teacher. However, if the teacher followed the instructions in the test manual and expressed the raw score of sixty-six as a grade level, or *grade equivalent* of 5.8, the *grade equivalent score* would be more meaningful to the teacher than

raw

the _____ score.

27. Besides providing instructions for expressing any given raw score as a grade equivalent score, standardized test manuals often provide other forms or indices of achievement by which raw

expressed

scores can be _____.

28. One other form, or index of achievement, by which any given raw score can be expressed, is a *centile score*. A raw score which is expressed as a centile score allows a teacher to determine where the score should be placed in relation to the percentage of the representative population who achieved a lower score. For example, if a child's raw score was expressed as a centile score, and if this score was placed at the sixtieth percentile, a teacher could conclude that the child's performance is equal to or better than the score

sixty

attained by _____ percent of the children in the representative population.

29. The two most common indices of achievement into which raw scores on standardized tests can

grade

be converted are _____ equivalent scores

centile

and _____ scores. Raw scores usually are converted into other indices of achievement

meaningful

because raw scores are not _____ for a teacher in comparing the test performance of his class with the test performance of a representative population.

30. For example, once a teacher had expressed a given raw score as a grade equivalent score or a centile score, the teacher would have a comparison of the score in relation to the performance of the representative population who had taken the same test. Consider a raw score that has been expressed as a grade equivalent score of 5.8. It could be said that, based upon the distribution of test scores in the representative population, the child would be performing on a level equal to that of a child in the eighth month of the

fifth

_____ grade.

31. Similarly, if a raw score is expressed as a centile score and if this centile score is found to be at

representative

the sixtieth percentile, a teacher could conclude that the child's performance was equal to or better than the score attained by 60% of the children in the ＿＿＿＿＿＿＿＿＿ population who had taken the same test.

32. Thus, when the information a teacher desires for an assessment of the achievement of his students includes a comparison with a large number of children in similar classes, a teacher can use the meaningful indices of achievement provided in

standardized

the manuals of ＿＿＿＿＿＿＿＿ tests.

33. On the other hand, if a teacher merely wanted to obtain information for a *subjective* comparison of the average achievement of his class with the average achievement of another similar class, he could use any informal teacher-made test. He could not accurately use such a test with confidence to compare his class objectively with a representative population, however, since his test would not include information about how

population

the representative ＿＿＿＿＿＿＿＿ might have performed on the test.

34. Standardized tests which assess general achievement in an area such as reading are called *survey tests,* since they survey a child's general reading abilities. If a teacher wanted to assess the general reading abilities of a child or a class in relation to the performance of a representative population, he would use a standardized

survey

＿＿＿＿＿＿＿＿ reading test.

35. If a teacher wanted to diagnose a child's mastery of *specific* skills, he probably would not use a standardized survey test, since a survey test measures only a child's ＿＿＿＿＿＿＿＿ achievement.

general

36. For example, a typical standardized survey test in reading might include a measure of a child's achievement in the major skill of reading comprehension. In an earlier lesson in this book, the skill of reading comprehension was shown to be comprised of several subskills. Generally, standardized survey tests designed to measure read-

subskills

ing comprehension measure only a few of the

_____ comprising the major skill of reading comprehension, but not all of these subskills.

37. To assess a child's mastery of specific skills with a standardized test, a teacher would use a standardized *diagnostic test*. Standardized diagnostic tests are designed to measure a child's specific reading abilities and are unlike most standardized survey tests which are designed to measure only

general

a child's _____ reading abilities.

38. In the area of reading comprehension, the major skill of reading comprehension might be assessed through the use of a standardized survey test. The subskills comprising the major skill might be assessed through the use of a standardized

diagnostic

_____ test.

39. A standardized diagnostic test differs from a standardized survey test in that a diagnostic test is

specific

designed to measure a child's _____ abilities, while a survey test is designed to assess

general

a child's _____ abilities.

PART TWO: Interpreting the Results of Tests

1. From the discussion of standardized tests to this point, it can be concluded correctly that a standardized test is merely a sample task which is designed to assess how well a person can perform a task he has been trained to do and which might include information about how well a similar population performed on the same material. For example, a standardized test in mathematics

mathematics

matics would be a sample task in _____.

2. Similarly, a standardized test in reading would

reading

be a sample task in _____.

3. It should be remembered, however, that since standardized tests are only sample tasks, the con-

tent of standardized tests constitutes only a *sample* of performance. Therefore, a teacher should exercise caution in evaluating total per-

sample

formance on the basis of a _____ of performance.

4. It also should be remembered that information provided about the performance of a representative population is merely a reporting of the achievement of people who took the test, not necessarily a *standard* of achievement toward which teachers should strive. For example, a teacher of a class of exceptionally capable children might be setting his sights too low if he used the performance of a representative pop-

standard

ulation as a _____ of achievement toward which his students should strive.

5. It is also possible that factors such as pupil tension, emotional or physical problems, and other factors related to a student's performance or to the testing situation could detract from the obtaining of a true picture of a child's ability. In interpreting the results of any standardized test, it is important for a teacher to consider any factors which might have influenced the

performance or achievement

_____ of a child on the test.

PART THREE: Kinds of Assessment

1. Despite the fact that caution must be exercised in interpreting the results of standardized tests, teachers can have confidence in several aspects of standardized tests. Since standardized tests include directions for administration, scoring, and use, a teacher seeking an objective method of comparing his class with a large number of classes could expect that other teachers who had administered a given standardized test had followed the specified directions for administration,

use

scoring, and _____.

2. Any assessment procedure which includes specific directions intended to guarantee that all teachers will complete the assessment procedure

in the same way is a part of *formal* assessment. Since standardized tests include specific directions for administration, scoring, and use, stan-

formal

dardized tests would be a part of _____ assessment.

formal

3. Observations by a teacher, however, would not be a part of _____ assessment, since all teachers probably would not observe children in the same way.

4. In formal assessment, the conditions under which information is obtained and classified are carefully controlled, and scores can be expressed in a form which will permit comparisons. In informal assessment, the conditions under which information is obtained are not necessarily care-

controlled

fully _____, and there is opportunity for subjective teacher judgment. If scores are used, they are not necessarily expressed in a form

comparisons

which will permit _____.

5. A test which is *not* administered, scored, and interpreted in strict accordance with specified conditions and which allows for subjective teacher judgment would be an example of

informal

_____ assessment.

6. A test which *is* administered, scored, and interpreted in strict accordance with specified conditions and which includes directions intended to minimize teacher subjective judgment would

formal

be an example of _____ assessment.

7. In informal assessment, a teacher might employ checklists, conferences, observations, workbook pages, teacher-made tests, or other methods of gathering information which do not necessarily require strict adherence to specified conditions. In formal assessment, a teacher would use

standardized

_____ tests which require strict adherence to specified conditions.

8. To compare a student's achievement with the achievement of other students in a class, or to

compare the achievement of one class with the achievement of a similar class, a teacher can use formal or informal assessment. To minimize subjective teacher judgment in comparing the achievement of a student or class with the achievement of a representative population,

standardized

however, a teacher would use _____

formal

tests, which are a part of _____ assessment.

9. To minimize subjective judgment in assessing a child's *general* achievement, a teacher would use a standardized survey test. To assess a child's *specific* abilities, a teacher would use a standard-

diagnostic

ized _____ test.

informal

10. Assessment, then, may be formal or _____. In formal assessment, a teacher can use standard-

diagnostic

ized survey tests or standardized _____ tests. Checklists, observations, workbook pages, conferences, teacher-made tests, and other methods of gathering information can be employed

informal

in _____ assessment. In establishing a successful program of reading instruction, it is important to include evaluation, diagnosis, measurement, and appraisal, all of which are a part

assessment

of the act of _____.

11. The effectiveness of methods, the appropriateness of materials, the achievement of children in a class, or other factors which might be directly or potentially related to the achieving of the objectives of a successful reading program should

assessment

be included in an _____ of the program.

12. It is likely that the factors identified as being either directly or potentially related to achieving objectives of a successful reading program will undergo continuous change. As changes in these factors occur, a change in the activities of the teacher also should occur. To adequately respond to change, a teacher should remember that since change is a continual process, assessment also

continual

should be a _____ process.

Review Questions

1. List several words which have been used synonymously with the word "assessment." (See Frame 2, Part One, to check your answer.)

2. In what forms are raw scores on standardized tests commonly expressed? (See Frames 26-28, Part One, to check your answer.)

3. Identify the two kinds of standardized tests described in this lesson. (See Frame 37, Part One, to check your answer.)

4. What type of activities are considered appropriate for informal assessment? (See Frame 10, Part Three, to check your answer.)

Informal Techniques of Assessment:
The Informal Reading Inventory

OBJECTIVE: Upon completion of parts One, Two, and Three, the reader will be able to:
1. describe how to construct, administer, and score Informal Reading Inventory;
2. define the terms *functional reading levels, independent level, instructional level, frustration level,* and *capacity level;*
3. list the types of word pronunciation errors recorded on the oral reading section of an informal reading inventory.

PART ONE: What Is the Informal Reading Inventory (IRI)?

1. In the previous lesson, it was pointed out that one important aspect of reading instruction is assessment. If a teacher can assess a child's strengths and deficiences in specific reading skills, the teacher can capitalize on the child's strengths and provide instruction and practice for the child in his deficiencies in these specific

skills   reading ——————.

2. If a teacher can *assess the level* at which a child can read successfully on his own, the teacher can also select books for a child at the appro-

level   priate —————— of difficulty.

3. Survey-type standardized achievement tests are frequently used for assessment. Although standardized achievement tests provide a maximal score or maximal level at which a child can read, it is not advisable to use this maximal level in

books or material   selecting —————— for a child to read on his own.

4. The reason why it is not advisable to use a child's maximal level of reading achievement on a standardized survey test in selecting books for a child

is that a child's reading achievement test score is often indicative of the level at which he becomes frustrated, or his *frustration level*. When frustration is experienced, optimal learning is impaired. Therefore, optimal learning will not likely occur if books are selected for a child on

frustration

a level which is close to his _____ level of reading achievement.

5. Books which can be read successfully by a child on his own are books which a child probably would read for recreation. Therefore, to select appropriate books for a child to read independently with success, it would be helpful for a teacher to know the level of reading at which a child reads for *recreation,* or his *recreational*

level

_____.

6. Since a child's recreational level of reading is the level at which a child reads on his own or the level at which he reads independently, the recreational level of reading is sometimes called the

level

independent _____ of reading.

7. Standardized tests provide information which can help a teacher estimate a child's probable frustration level of reading but they do not provide information about a child's recreational, or

independent

_____ level of reading.

8. In some instances, a child who cannot read material successfully on his own can read material successfully with minimal instruction from the teacher. While administering a standardized achievement test, however, a teacher is not allowed to provide instruction to assist a child in successfully completing portions of the test, other than providing directions included in the test. Therefore, standardized survey tests do not provide information about a child's *instructional level* of reading, which is the level at which a

instruction or help

child can read successfully with _____ from the teacher.

9. It is probable that there are many concepts which a child has the capacity to understand when

someone reads them to him, but which he cannot understand if he has to read them by himself. When a child reads material by himself, it is difficult to determine the level of his *capacity* to understand, since limited word attack skills or other factors may prevent him from understanding concepts which he would understand in an oral context. However, a child's capacity to understand material presented orally, or his *capac-*

level

ity _____, can be assessed through reading material to the child and by checking his understanding of concepts presented.

10. Questions found in survey-type standardized achievement tests elicit responses related to material which a child has read by himself. Therefore, standardized tests ordinarily do not provide information about the level at which the child has the *capacity* to understand the material to which he listens. This level is often called the *listening level* as well as the capacity

level

_____.

11. Of the three levels of reading ability — independent level, instructional level, and frustration level — as well as the capacity (listening) level of understanding orally–presented material, standardized survey tests usually provide information

frustration

which is indicative of a child's _____

**independent or
recreational,
instructional**

level. Some other method of assessment must be used to obtain information about the other three

levels, the _____ level, the _____

capacity

level, and the _____ level.

12. The *Informal Reading Inventory* is a method of assessment which has been used successfully to determine a child's various reading levels and his level of understanding of orally presented material. Unlike standardized tests, which usually provide information indicative of a child's

frustration

_____ level of reading, the Informal Reading Inventory provides information which assists the teacher in determining all three

levels

_____ of a child's reading achievement as well as his level of understanding of orally–presented materials.

13. The three levels of reading achievement — independent, instructional, and frustration — and the capacity level of understanding provided by the Informal Reading Inventory are based on *minimum percentages of accuracy* which must be achieved by a child in two aspects of reading in materials of varying levels of difficulty: word pronunciation and comprehension in an oral reading selection and comprehension in a silent

selection

reading _____.

14. The three levels of reading achievement and the listening capacity level are listed below. Beside each level of achievement are the minimum percentages of accuracy in word pronunciation and comprehension which must be attained by a child in selected materials, in order to determine any of his levels of performance. You may wish to refer to this information in completing several of the following frames:

WORD PRONUNCIATION
and COMPREHENSION

Level	Word Pronunciation (Oral Reading)	Comprehension (Oral and Silent Reading)
Independent Reading Level	98%	90%
Instructional Reading Level	95%	75%
Frustration Level	90%	50%
Capacity Level		75%

Suppose, for example, that a child reads an oral selection and a silent selection which have been graded at the 3-1 (third grade, first book) level of difficulty. In order to say that the child's independent reading level is the 3-1 level or higher, the teacher would have to know that a child achieved

98

minimum percentages of _____ _____% accu-

90

racy in word pronunciation, and _____% accuracy in comprehension.

15. If a child attained these minimum percentages at the 3-1 level, the teacher could then provide a selection graded at the 3-2 level of difficulty. At this level, if the child did not achieve minimum percentages of accuracy of 98% in word pronunciation and 90% in comprehension, the teacher would then conclude that the 3-2 level of difficulty is not the child's _____ reading level, since the minimum percentages of accuracy established for this level were not attained.

independent

16. The highest level at which the minimum percentages of accuracy established for the *independent* reading level were attained was the 3-1 level of difficulty. Therefore, the teacher could conclude that the 3-1 level of difficulty is the child's ____ ____ reading level, or the level at which the child can read independently without marked difficulty.

independent

17. Suppose, however, that at the 3-2 level of difficulty the child achieved 96% accuracy in word pronunciation and 85% accuracy in comprehension. These percentages, although they are lower than the minimum percentages established for the *independent* reading level, are *higher* than the minimum percentages established for the _____ reading level.

instructional

18. Since the percentages are *higher* than the minimum percentages of accuracy established for the *instructional* reading level, the teacher could conclude that level 3-2 or higher would be the child's _____ reading level.

instructional

19. The teacher could then direct the child to read selections graded at increasing levels of difficulty until the minimum percentages of accuracy established for the *instructional* reading level were no longer attained. The highest level of difficulty at which the minimum percentages of accuracy were attained by the child would then be the child's probable instructional reading _____.

level

20. Suppose that a child attained 96% accuracy in word pronunciation and 80% accuracy in comprehension at the 3-2 level. Suppose further that he continued to read in materials of increasing difficulty and attained not less than 95% accuracy in word pronunciation and 75% accuracy in comprehension at the fourth and fifth grade levels. Suppose, though, that at the *sixth* grade level he attained 96% accuracy in word pronunciation, but *only 70%* accuracy in comprehension. This child's instructional reading level would be the highest level at which he had attained *both* minimum percentages of accuracy established for

instructional
the _____ reading level.

21. The minimum percentages of accuracy for the instructional reading level are 95% accuracy in word pronunciation and 75% accuracy in comprehension. The highest level at which the child attained percentages of accuracy which were *not lower* than these percentages was

fifth
the _____ grade level.

22. The probable instructional reading level of the child referred to above would be the

fifth
_____ grade level.

23. After determining the areas in which a child is reading at his independent reading level and his instructional reading level, a teacher is knowledgeable concerning the point at which the next

frustration
level — the child's _____ reading level — begins.

24. In the case of the child above, the highest level at which he attained the minimum percentages of accuracy established for the instructional reading level was the fifth grade. He did *not* attain these minimum percentages of accuracy at the sixth grade level. Therefore, a teacher would know that the point at which this child's frustra-

sixth
tion reading level begins is the _____ grade level.

25. Any percentages of accuracy below 95% in word pronunciation or 75% accuracy in comprehen-

sion would be suggestive of a child's probable

frustration

_____ level of reading.

26. Factors such as a child's interest in the material he is reading can affect a child's performance in reading the material. Therefore, even though a teacher can determine that his probable frustration level begins at the point at which he can no longer attain minimum percentages of accuracy of 95% in word pronunciation and 75% accuracy in comprehension, a teacher could have a child continue to read until he could no longer attain minimum percentages of accuracy of 90% in word pronunciation and 50% in comprehension. These percentages of accuracy are the minimum percentages established for the

frustration

_____ level of reading.

27. Suppose that a child attained 92% accuracy in word pronunciation and 60% accuracy in comprehension at the seventh grade level of difficulty. However, suppose that at the eighth grade level of difficulty he attained only 80% accuracy in word pronunciation and only 40% accuracy in comprehension. These percentages are lower than the minimum percentages established for the _frustration_ reading level. Therefore, a teacher would probably no longer expect the child to

read

_____ the material by himself.

28. It should be pointed out that when a child fails to attain the minimum percentages of accuracy established for the _instructional_ reading level, the grade level of difficulty of the material he is reading would be _indicative_ of his frustration level of reading. Minimum percentages of accuracy are helpful in determining when a child is reading at his frustration level; however, a teacher should be alert to nervousness, fidgeting, tension, word-by-word reading, frowning, or other signs of

frustration or tension

_____ .

29. _Teacher judgment_ based on careful observation during the testing situation, then, should be used in conjunction with the minimum percentages of accuracy in determining a child's various

levels

_____ of reading ability.

frustration

30. For example, even though a child might attain minimum percentages of accuracy of 96% and 80% on material graded at the fifth grade level of difficulty, if behaviors such as poor phrasing, extreme tension, or excessive nervousness suddenly became apparent at this level, it probably would be accurate to conclude that the material is closer to the child's _____ reading level than it is to his instructional reading level.

capacity

31. When a child's independent reading level, his instructional reading level, and his frustration reading level have been established, the teacher can next attempt to determine the child's _____ _____ level.

capacity

32. Earlier in this chapter, it was pointed out that a child's capacity level is his ability to understand material read to him by the teacher. Since the teacher would no longer expect a child to read when he fails to attain at least 90% accuracy in word pronunciation and 50% accuracy in comprehension, the remaining selections must be read to the child by the teacher if the child's _____ level is to be determined.

eighth

33. In the example cited above, the highest level at which the child attained the minimum percentages of accuracy for the frustration reading level was the seventh grade level of difficulty. Thus, the teacher would begin to assess the child's capacity level by reading to him, starting with material at the _____ grade level of difficulty, since the child did not attain the minimum percentages of accuracy at the eighth grade level of difficulty.

34. A child's capacity level is the level at which he must achieve a minimum percentage of accuracy of 75% in comprehension of material read to him by the teacher, as well as being able to converse fluently with the teacher in terminology on the level of difficulty of the material under discussion. If the highest level at which a child converses fluently and achieves 75% accuracy in comprehension of material read to him is the

tenth grade level of difficulty, the tenth grade
level of difficulty would be indicative of the

capacity   child's _____ level.

35. Knowledge of a child's three levels of ability in
reading — his *functional reading levels*—and his
level of ability to understand what is read for him
can be of immense assistance to a teacher. For
example, if a teacher knows that a child's independent reading level is the 3-1 level of difficulty, the teacher can help the child select recreational reading materials which would be graded

difficulty   at about the 3-1 level of _____.

36. Since a teacher usually provides instruction to
build background or to preview difficult concepts
which a child might encounter in reading text-
book assignments, a teacher can provide instructional materials and textbooks which are graded
at a level of difficulty which corresponds with a

instructional   child's _____ reading level.

37. A teacher who knows a child's frustration level
would avoid assigning reading material which is
graded at a level of difficulty which corresponds

frustration   with the child's _____ level, since optimal learning is impaired when excessive frustra-
tion is experienced.

38. Teachers frequently provide instruction orally
that deals with concepts which children have the
capacity to understand, but which they often lack
the ability to read on their own. For purposes of
oral instruction, a teacher can judge the level of
difficulty of a concept which a child might be
able to understand by assessing the child's

capacity   _____ level.

PART TWO: Constructing the Informal Reading Inventory

1. In the Informal Reading Inventory a child's functional reading levels and his capacity to understand orally-presented material are established on
the basis of his proficiency in reading and listening to material which has been graded according to readability. Basal reading series are, there-

fore, a convenient source from which a teacher can obtain graded reading selections, since it is common for basal readers to be graded accord-

readability

ing to _ _____.

2. Since a child must demonstrate his reading proficiency at various levels of difficulty in word pronunciation and comprehension on oral reading selections and in comprehension on silent reading selections, a teacher would choose two selections from each graded reader — a selection to be read orally and a selection to be read

silently

_____.

3. On the word pronunciation assessment, a child is assessed on his ability to pronounce words. On the comprehension assessment, however, the teacher will have to provide questions for the child to answer, since the child's ability to comprehend the material he reads is assessed by de-

questions

termining how well he can answer_____ about the material.

4. In an earlier lesson, it was pointed out that comprehension is based, in part, on the reader's ability to remember facts, to draw inference, to understand vocabulary, and to use context clues. If these factors are indicative of a child's reading comprehension, the questions a teacher asks a child in order to assess his reading comprehension should be questions which assess the re-

inference

membering of facts, the drawing of _____,

vocabulary

the understanding of _____, and the

context

ability to use _____ clues.

5. A convenient number of questions to use for each oral and silent reading selection would be about five to seven questions. In constructing the questions, the teacher should strive to achieve a balance among questions of fact, questions of

inference, vocabulary

_____, questions of _____,
and questions requiring the ability to use

context

_____ clues.

6. In many basal readers, the first part of each book

— about one-third of the book — is written at the level of the preceding grade. The material which is graded at the level of difficulty indicated by the number or symbol on each book usually begins after the first one-third of the book. Therefore, an appropriate place from which to select material for oral and silent reading would be the part of the book immediately following the first

one-third or third

_____ of the book.

7. Selections from the pre-primer levels, the primer level, and the first and second grade levels should be about 60-125 words long. Selections from levels three, four, five, and six should be about 100-200 words long. As the selections become greater in difficulty, they should also become

length

greater in _____ .

PART THREE: Administering and Scoring the Informal Reading Inventory

1. When a child experiences *success* in a task, he is usually willing to undertake another task of a similar nature. Since the IRI consists of a series of tasks of a similar nature, in order to ensure the willingness of a child to participate further, it is

success

important that the child experience _____ in his first reading task on the IRI.

2. The teacher administering the IRI should determine a level of reading at which a child can experience success. He should then start the child

level

at this _____ when administering the IRI.

3. After establishing a beginning level at which success is probable for a child, the teacher should provide only such background as is necessary to establish a logical beginning point for the reading of a selection and then direct the child to

read

_____ the selection orally.

4. As the child reads the selection from the reader, the teacher keeps a record of the child's errors on a separate copy of the selection. The teacher records the number of errors and the kinds of errors the child makes in word pronunciation on

oral

the _____ reading selection.

5. The teacher also records the number of errors the child makes in responding to comprehension

oral

questions on the _____ reading selec-

silent

tion, and on the _____ reading selection.

6. In oral reading, there are several different kinds of errors a child might make. For example, a child might make an error of *substitution*. This kind of

substitutes

error would occur when a child _____ one or more words for another word or words.

7. A child might make other kinds of errors, such as omitting, inserting, or repeating words. He also might mispronounce words or refuse to pronounce them at all. When testing a child in oral reading, the teacher records any of the above

kinds or types

_____ of errors a child might make.

8. In oral reading, if a child *substitutes* the word *black* for the word *back,* for example, the teacher would record this kind of error as an error of

substitution

_____.

9. An error of substitution occurs when one or more words are substituted for another word or words. An error of *omission* occurs when one or more

omitted or left out

words are _____ by a child.

10. An error of *mispronunciation* occurs when a child

mispronounces

_____ a word. An error of *repetition*

repeats

occurs when a child _____ two or more words.

11. In instances where a child refuses to pronounce a word after a five second delay, the teacher would pronounce the word for the child. An error

refuses

of *refusal* occurs when a child _____ to pronounce a word.

12. If a child disregards punctuation while reading a selection, his *disregard of punctuation* would be

kind or type

recorded as an additional _____ of error which might be made in oral reading.

13. Only one error at any place in the reading is counted. Thus, if a child makes an error of substitution and then repeats a phrase to correct the error of substitution, the error is counted as either an error of substitution or an error of repetition. If the error is recorded as an error of substitution,

repetition

it is *not* also recorded as an error of _____.

14. An omission of two or three words in a row would be another example of an error occurring at only one place in the reading that is counted as only one error. Similarly, an insertion of two or three words in a row would be counted as only

one

_____ error.

15. In basic sight word substitution, however, it is common practice for a teacher to count such an error each time it occurs, since repeated errors of this type would be indicative of a child's inability to use context clues. Therefore, if a child substitutes the word "then" for the word "when" in three different places, the substitution error

three

should be counted as _____ (how many?) errors.

16. Mispronunciations of proper nouns or foreign words often are not counted as errors. If a child mispronounces the proper noun "Colorado" as "Columbia," for example, the teacher would not

error

count the mispronunciation as an _____, since word attack skills frequently have limited application in relation to proper nouns or foreign words.

17. A record of the kinds of errors a child makes can be of value to the teacher in planning specific instructional exercises for a child. The *number* of errors a child makes in word pronunciation and in comprehension is important to the teacher

accuracy

in computing percentages of _____ in each of the areas tested by the Informal Reading Inventory.

18. Once the percentages of accuracy have been determined, the teacher can tentatively identify the child's functional reading levels and his ability to understand orally-presented material. The identification of these various levels of ability was identified earlier in this chapter as a major purpose to be accomplished in administering the

Reading Inventory | Informal _____ _____ .

Review Questions

1. The Informal Reading Inventory can be used to establish a child's probable functional reading levels as well as his capacity (listening) level. Briefly describe each of the levels listed below:

   a. independent reading level (See Frame 6, Part One, to check your answer.)

   b. instructional reading level (See Frame 8, Part One, to check your answer.)

   c. frustration reading level (See Frame 4, Part One, to check your answer.)

   d. capacity level (See Frame 9, Part One, to check your answer.)

2. Briefly describe the main points a teacher would need to keep in mind in constructing an Informal Reading Inventory. (See Frames 2-7, Part Two, to check your answer.)

3. Identify as many of the different kinds of oral reading errors as you can that a teacher might need to record in administering an Informal Reading Inventory. (See Frames 6-13, Part Three, to check your answer.)

Informal Techniques of Assessment:
The Cloze Test Procedure

OBJECTIVE: Upon completion of Parts One through Four, the reader will be able to construct, administer, and score a cloze test, and describe the advantages and limitations of the cloze test.

PART ONE: What Is the Cloze Test?

1. Although the Informal Reading Inventory (IRI) discussed in the previous lesson is a helpful tool in the assessment of a child's functional reading levels, the IRI usually poses several problems for a beginning teacher. One problem is that a certain amount of skill in constructing an IRI is required if a teacher-constructed IRI is used. A beginning teacher might not feel that he pos-

skill

    sesses this necessary _____ to approach the task of constructing an IRI.

2. An example of the kind of problem a beginning teacher might face would be the problem of constructing appropriate questions for an IRI. For example, if a beginning teacher has difficulty identifying a question of inference from a list of several questions, it would not be likely that he would feel confident constructing a question

inference

    of _____.

3. A certain amount of teacher skill also is required in administering an IRI. For example, one aspect of administering an IRI which requires skill is the recording of the number and kinds of oral reading errors a child makes. In considering this challenge, a beginning teacher might not feel that

administer

    he possesses the necessary skill to _____ an IRI accurately.

4. Since the IRI usually is given as an individual test, a teacher must be prepared to devote a consid-

erable amount of time to administering the IRI, especially if he decides to use it to assess the abilities of all students in his class. Since a teacher usually finds himself with less time than with any

time

other commodity, the amount of _____ required for an IRI might pose an additional problem for a beginning teacher.

5. Although the information provided by the IRI is a valuable aid to a teacher in planning instruction, a beginning teacher might decide that because of problems, such as the desirability of a certain amount of skill in constructing and administering an IRI, the extensive time involved

problems or factors

in administering it, or other such _____, the IRI would not be a feasible tool for him to use in his assessment program.

6. An alternative tool for assessment which does not present a beginning teacher with the problems posed by the IRI is the *Cloze Test*. Besides presenting a teacher with fewer problems than an IRI, a Cloze Test differs from the IRI in that it does not provide information about a child's word pronunciation abilities in oral reading. A Cloze Test *does* provide information about a child's functional reading levels and, in this re-

IRI

spect, it is similar to an _____.

7. It will be remembered that, in using an IRI, a teacher could determine a child's independent, instructional, and frustration reading levels. Similarly, in using a Cloze Test, a teacher can determine a child's independent, instructional, and

levels

frustration reading _____.

8. A Cloze Test, then, can be partially defined as simply a test which can be used to determine a

reading

child's functional _____ levels.

PART TWO: Constructing the Cloze Test

1. A child's functional reading levels are determined on a Cloze Test by the *percentage of accuracy* with which he can supply words that have been

deleted from passages of varying levels of difficulty. A first step in constructing a Cloze Test
is the selecting of passages of varying levels of

difficulty

_____.

2. Since a child's functional reading levels usually
are given a grade-level designation, the passages
selected for a Cloze Test also should be given a

grade

_____ level designation.

3. Once a teacher has selected passages which have
been given a grade-level designation, he must
then delete selected words from the passages,
since, as Frame 1 of this section pointed out, a
child's functional reading levels are determined
on a Cloze Test by the percentage of accuracy

words

with which he can supply missing _____
that have been deleted from passages.

4. Several different recommendations have been
made regarding the number of words to be deleted and the intervals at which words should
be deleted. One formula which has been used
successfully involves the deleting of every fifth
word in a passage, excluding words in the first
sentence which is left intact. A second step in
constructing a Cloze Test is the deleting of every

fifth

_____ word in each passage, exclusive
of the words in the first sentence in each passage.

5. After deleting every fifth word, the teacher fills
each space with a standard length blank; that is,
each deleted word is replaced with a blank of
the same length. The word "the," for example,
would be replaced with a blank of the same

length

_____ as, say, the word "constitution."

6. In Cloze Tests which follow the formula of deleting every fifth word, passages containing approxi-
mately fifty deletions have been found to be
accurate in assessing a child's functional reading
levels. A typical passage on a Cloze Test, there-

250 (every fifth word
× 50 deletions =
5 × 50)

fore, should be *about* _____ words long,
exclusive of the first sentence.

7. A summary of the procedure to be followed in constructing a Cloze Test would be the following:

   a. Select passages of about 260-275 words which have been given grade-_____ designations.

level

   b. Leave the first _____ of each passage intact.

sentence

   c. After the first sentence, delete every _____ word.

fifth

   d. Replace each word with a standard length _____.

blank

PART THREE: Administering and Scoring the Cloze Test

1. A child's functional reading levels on a Cloze Test are determined by the percentages of accuracy with which he can supply the *exact* missing words which have been deleted from selected passages. In administering a Cloze Test a teacher would provide a child with a passage from which selected words have been _____.

deleted

2. After the child has been provided with a passage on a level of difficulty at which the teacher feels he will not be frustrated, the teacher instructs the child to fill in the blanks with the exact missing _____ which the child thinks might have been in the blanks before the words were deleted.

words

3. There is no time limit on a Cloze Test; therefore, a teacher would allow a child sufficient _____ to complete a given passage.

time

4. In scoring a Cloze Test, a teacher simply counts the number of correct responses made by the child. A response is counted as correct only if the *exact* word which was present in the original passage has been provided, disregarding minor misspellings. Therefore, even if a child were to supply an excellent synonym for a deleted word, the

exact

response would *not* be counted as a correct response, since the synonym would not be the

_____ word which was present in the original passage.

5. Once the correct number of responses has been tabulated, a child's score is converted into a percentage. For example, if a child supplies the exact words for twenty-five of fifty deletions, the child's raw score, 25/50, would be converted to

a percentage score of _____ percent.

$$\frac{50}{50 \overline{\smash{)}25.000}}$$

6. A child's percentage of accuracy in responding then would be compared to the percentage of accuracy which has been established for each of

reading

the functional _____ levels.

7. The three functional reading levels have been listed below. Beside each level is a selected percentage of accuracy which can be used as a minimum percentage a child must attain before it can be determined that he is functioning at any given level.

Accuracy in Supplying
Deleted Words in a
Given Passage

Independent Reading Level	57%
Instructional Reading Level	44-57%
Frustration Level	Below 44%

Suppose, for example, that a child supplies missing words from a passage for which a grade-level designation of fifth grade has been established. In order to say that the child's independent reading level is fifth grade or higher, a teacher would have to know that the child has supplied at least

57

_____ % of the exact words which had been deleted.

8. If a child supplies at least 57% of the exact words which have been deleted from a passage desig-

nated as being of fifth grade difficulty, the teacher might then supply a passage designated as sixth grade difficulty. If the child does *not* achieve at least 57% accuracy in supplying exact deleted words at this level, the teacher could conclude that the sixth grade level is probably not the

independent

child's _____ reading level, since the minimum percentage of accuracy established for the independent reading level has not been attained.

9. Further, suppose that the fifth grade level was the highest grade level at which the minimum percentage of accuracy established for the independent reading level was attained. A teacher could then conclude that the fifth grade level of difficulty would be indicative of the child's

independent

_____ – reading level.

10. Suppose, though, that the child has attained a minimum percentage of accuracy of 50% at the sixth grade level of difficulty. The teacher could then conclude that the sixth grade level or higher would be indicative of the child's instructional reading level, since his percentage of accuracy

44

was higher than a percentage of _____%, a percentage established as the minimum for the instructional reading level.

11. The teacher might then direct the child to complete a Cloze Test on material graded at the seventh grade level of difficulty. If a child attains a percentage of accuracy of less than 44% at the seventh grade level, the teacher would conclude that the child's instructional reading level would

seventh

probably not be _____ grade, since the child failed to attain the minimum percentage of accuracy established for the instructional reading level.

12. The highest level at which the child attained a minimum percentage of accuracy of 44% was the sixth grade level. Therefore, the teacher would conclude that the sixth grade level was

instructional

indicative of the child's _____ level and that, since the child achieved below 44% accuracy at the seventh grade level, the seventh grade level would be indicative of the child's

frustration

_____ level.

13. In summary, any percentage of accuracy below 44% in supplying exact words which have been deleted from a given passage would be indicative of a child's

frustration

tive of a child's _____ level.

14. Further, any percentage of accuracy between 44% and 57% would be indicative of a child's

instructional

_____ reading level.

15. A child's independent reading level would be the level at which he could supply the exact missing words with a minimum percentage of

57

accuracy of _____ %.

PART FOUR: Advantages and Limitations of the Cloze Test

1. Although graded passages are used in establishing a child's functional reading levels, a Cloze Test can also be constructed with passages from material which has not been graded, if a teacher merely wants to know whether a particular book is appropriate for a particular child. For example, a teacher might want to use a particular book for instruction in social studies. He could then construct a Cloze Test with passages selected from the book, establish a child's percentages of accuracy, and determine whether the book is at

instructional

the child's _____ reading level.

2. In this case, if the child attains a percentage of accuracy of 52% on a passage selected from a particular book, the teacher could conclude that this book—or perhaps a more difficult book—

instructional

would be at the child's _____ reading level.

3. Without knowing the graded level of difficulty of a more difficult book containing topics consistent with his objectives in social studies, the teacher could construct a second Cloze Test. If

the child's percentage of accuracy in the more difficult book was below 44%, the teacher could determine that the first book he had chosen was at the child's instructional reading level; therefore, even though he might not know the graded

level

_____ of difficulty of the book, the teacher could select an appropriate book for instruction.

4. A Cloze Test, then, can be used to determine whether materials are appropriate for instruction for a child, even though grade levels have not been established for the materials. A Cloze Test can also be used to determine a child's functional reading levels, based on his performance on materials for which grade levels *have* been

established or
determined

_____.

5. Another advantage of the Cloze Test is that un-like the IRI, which requires substantial skills on the part of a teacher in its construction and administration, the Cloze Test requires very few

construction,
administration

skills in its _____ and _____.

6. Further, since a Cloze Test can be administered to a total group in a relatively short period of time, an added advantage of the Cloze Test over

time

the IRI would be that it requires less _____ to construct and administer than is required with the IRI.

7. A limitation inherent in the Cloze Test which is not found in the IRI is that the Cloze Test assesses only a child's functional reading levels in a silent reading situation, while the IRI assesses functional reading levels and the listening

capacity

_____ level, as well as the accuracy of word pronunciation skills.

Review Exercise

1. A passage from which a Cloze Test might be constructed has been provided below. Applying your knowledge of how to construct a Cloze Test, construct a Cloze Test from this passage that describes

sites to visit in Washington, D.C. Then compare the test you have constructed with the test which appears below.

Perhaps you will enjoy a visit to the United States Treasury Building. Here are kept records of all government money received from taxes, or paid out for any government expense. Officers in this building oversee the running of all national banks in the country. From the Treasury Building, all United States paper money is issued, and to it old, worn-out bills are sent to be exchanged and destroyed. You will see the White House, our President's home, with its sloping lawns and lovely gardens. You will see the fine houses where representatives from other countries live while they are in Washington.

The Washington Monument is over 500 feet high. Its name tells you that it was built in honor of our first President. Visitors may reach the top of it by an elevator. From it, they can see far beyond the city in all directions.

The Lincoln Memorial is among the best known of the national shrines, or monuments. An old Negro guide who was showing visitors about the city said, "People will tell you that the Lincoln Memorial is the most beautiful thing in Washington, but I am sure it is the most beautiful thing in the world." This expresses the feeling of many Americans for this building which honors one of our country's greatest men.

Another beautiful memorial building, newly erected, is that to Thomas Jefferson, third President of our United States, and author of the Declaration of Independence.

At Arlington, across the Potomac from Washington, is beautiful Arlington National Cemetery. It contains the graves of hundreds of American soldiers and sailors and of many great statesmen.[1]

A CLOZE TEST

Perhaps you will enjoy a visit to the United States Treasury Building.

Here are kept records _____ all government money re-

ceived _____ taxes, or paid out _____ any gov-

ernment expenses. Officers _____ this building oversee the

_____ of all national banks _____ the country.

[1]From Ernest L. Thurston and Grace C. Hankins, *Homeland of the Americas* (Syracuse, New York: Iroquois Publishing Company, Inc., 1958), p. 90. Reprinted by permission of Charles E. Merrill Publishing Company.

From the _____ Building, all United States _____ money is issued, and _____ it old, worn-out _____ are sent to be _____ and destroyed. You will _____ the White House, our _____ home, with its sloping _____ and lovely gardens. You _____ see the fine houses _____ representatives from other countries _____ while they are in _____.

The Washington Monument is _____ 500 feet high. Its _____ tells you that it _____ built in honor of _____ first President. Visitors may _____ the top of it _____ an elevator. From it, _____ can see far beyond _____ city in all directions.

_____ Lincoln Memorial is among _____ best known of the _____ shrines, or monuments. An _____ Negro guide who was _____ visitors about the city _____, "People will tell you _____ the Lincoln Memorial is _____ most beautiful thing in _____ but I am sure _____ is the most beautiful _____ in the world." This _____ the feeling of many _____ for this building which _____ one of our country's _____ men.

Another beautiful memorial _____ newly erected, is that _____ Thomas Jefferson, third President _____ our United States and _____ of the Declaration of _____.

At Arlington, across the _____ from Washington, is beautiful _____ National Cemetery. It contains _____ graves of hundreds of _____ soldiers and sailors and _____ many great statesmen.

2. Assume that a child has completed the Cloze Test on the previous page and that his responses have been duplicated in the sample below. Compare the child's responses with the original passage and then assess your ability in completing the following tasks: (answers follow the exercise.)

    a. Find the child's raw score.
    b. Convert the raw score to a percent.
    c. Identify the functional reading level at which the child is performing on the test by underlining one of the following:

        independent
        instructional
        frustration.

Perhaps you will enjoy a visit to the United States Treasury Building. Here are kept records *concerning* all government money received *in* taxes, or paid out *from* any government expense. Officers *at* this building oversee the *running* of all national banks *of* the country. From the *Trea-sury* Building, all United States *paper* money is issued, and *from* it old, worn-out *dollars* are sent to be *burned* and destroyed. You will *notice* the White House, our *President's* home, with its sloping *grass* and lovely gardens. You *will* see the fine houses *where* representatives from other countries *stay* while they are in *America*.

The Washington Monument is *eggsakly* 500 feet high. Its *sign* tells you that it *was* built in honor of *our* first President. Visitors may *see* the top of it *from* an elevator. From it, *you* can see far beyond *the* city in all directions.

The Lincoln Memorial is among *the* best known of the *nashional* shrines, or monuments. An *old* Negro guide who was *guiding* visitors about the city *stated*, "People will tell you *that* the Lincoln Memorial is *the* most beautiful thing in *America*, but I am sure ___*this*___ is the most beautiful ___*thing*___ in the world." This ___*tells*___ the feeling of many ___*people*___ for this building which ___*praises*___ one of our country's ___*best*___ men.

Another beautiful memorial ___*stone*___ newly erected, is that ___*for*___ Thomas Jefferson, third President ___*of*___ our United States and ___*writer*___ of the Declaration of *Independence*.

At Arlington, across the ___*bridge*___ from Washington, is beautiful *Washington* National Cemetery. It contains ___*many*___ graves of hundreds of ___*American*___ soldiers and sailors and ___*of*___ many great statesmen.

A Corrected Cloze Test

Perhaps you will enjoy a visit to the United States Treasury Building. Here are kept records *concerning* all government money received ___*in*___ taxes, or paid out ___*from*___ any government expense. Officers ___*at*___ this building oversee the *running* C of all national banks ___*of*___ the country. From the *Treasury* C Building, all United States ___*paper*___ C money is issued, and ___*from*___ it old, worn-out ___*dollars*___ are sent to be ___*burned*___ and destroyed. You will ___*notice*___ the White House, our *President's* C home, with its sloping ___*grass*___ and lovely gardens. You ___*will*___ C see the fine houses ___*where*___ C representatives from other countries ___*stay*___ while they are in *America*.

The Washington Monument is ___*eggsakly*___ 500 feet high. Its ___*sign*___ tells you that it ___*was*___ C built in honor of ___*our*___ C first President. Visitors may ___*see*___ the top of it __*from*__ an elevator. From it, __*you*__ can see far beyond __*the*__ **C** city in all directions.

__*the*__ **C** Lincoln Memorial is among __*the*__ **C** best known of the __*nashional*__ **C** shrines, or monuments. An __*old*__ **C** Negro guide who was __*guiding*__ visitors about the city __*stated*__ "People will tell you __*that*__ **C** the Lincoln Memorial is __*the*__ **C** most beautiful thing in __*America*__, but I am sure __*this*__ is the most beautiful __*thing*__ **C** in the world." This __*tells*__ the feeling of many __*people*__ for this building which __*praises*__ one of our country's __*best*__ men.

Another beautiful memorial __*stone*__, newly erected, is that __*for*__ Thomas Jefferson, third President __*of*__ **C** our United States and __*writer*__ of the Declaration of __*Independence.*__ **C**

At Arlington, across the __*bridge*__ from Washington, is beautiful __*Washington*__ National Cemetery. It contains __*many*__ graves of hundreds of __*American*__ **C** soldiers and sailors and __*of*__ **C** many great statesmen.

   a. Raw Score: twenty right answers.
   b. Percentage: thirty-nine percent ($20/51 = 51\overline{)20.00} = .392$
                     $= .39 =$ thirty-nine percent);
   c. The probable functional reading level is the *frustration* reading level, since the child failed to attain a percentage of accuracy of forty-four percent established as the minimum for the instructional reading level, or a percentage of accuracy of fifty-seven percent established as the minimum for the independent reading level. Had the child attained a percentage of forty-eight percent, it would not be accurate to conclude that his instructional reading level would be at the level of difficulty of this passage. It is possible that, given a more difficult passage at the higher level, he could still attain a

percentage of accuracy above the minimum percentage established for the instructional reading level. It then would be appropriate to give him another Cloze Test based on a selection from the next higher level of difficulty.

Grouping for Instruction in Reading

OBJECTIVE: The reader will be able to describe the two main principles of grouping for instruction, and define what is meant by the terms *homogeneous group* and *heterogeneous group.*

A large group has been described in the situation presented below. The large group can be subdivided into smaller groups in which the members have certain characteristics in common. (An example of a subgroup formed from the large group described below might be "males-females.")

Divide the large group into as many subgroups as possible. List the subgroups in the *most logical order* in the box on the following page:

On a certain ranch in eastern Colorado there is a large herd of cattle. Some of the cattle are males and some are females. Among the males, there are both steers and bulls. Among the females, some cattle can be found which do not give milk. A part of the herd is comprised of calves. The cattle in the herd are either black or brown. All of the cattle with horns are brown, but not all of the brown cattle have horns. A part of the herd is made up of dairy cattle; the other part of the herd is made up of beef cattle. The cattle in the herd are from Texas, Wyoming, and Colorado. Some of the cattle are fed hay, and some of the cattle are on green grass. Not all of the cattle from Colorado have eaten green grass.

The rancher has asked you, a beginning cowboy, to divide the herd into as many subgroups as possible (on paper) according to what you consider to be the most logical or most important order. The rancher will base his decision regarding your possible permanent employment on how well you do the job. (Assume that you need the job.)

Allow yourself five minutes to work on the problem above. Then turn to Frame 1 on the next page to check your answers. Proceed from Frame 1 and complete the remaining frames.

Subgroups

1. Regardless of how you grouped the cattle, you cannot be sure that you grouped them in the most logical order, since you did not know the rancher's purpose for grouping the cattle. In order to group wisely, you have to know the

purpose _____ for grouping.

2. If the rancher's primary purpose was to have his cattle grouped on the criterion of whether or not they had horns, you would not form your final groups on the basis of their color, because this criterion would be totally unrelated to the

purpose rancher's _____.

3. If, on the other hand, the rancher's primary purpose was to group all of his black cattle to ship them to market, you would first group the cattle

color on the basis of their _____, since you would be grouping them according to the

purpose rancher's primary _____, that of sending all of his black cattle to market.

4. It can be seen that without a knowledge of what the purpose is for grouping, logical grouping is impossible. Therefore, the most important principle to follow in grouping is to determine the

purpose _____ for establishing groups.

5. Any group in which the members of the group have been selected on the basis of some common characteristic or characteristics is called a *homogeneous* group. In the group of black cattle, color

was a *common characteristic* shared by all of the group members. Therefore, in reference to color, the group of black cattle could be called a

homogeneous

_____ group.

6. A group of horned cattle also could be called a

homogeneous

_____ group, in reference to the fact that all of the members of the group would have horns. In this group, the horns would be the

characteristic

common _____ shared by all the members of the group.

7. Where there is no attempt to select members for a group on the basis of some common characteristic or characteristics, the result is usually a group called a *heterogeneous* group. Other than the fact that the group members were all cattle, the large group of cattle which you attempted to divide into subgroups was not selected on the basis of some common characteristic; therefore, the large group of cattle would be called a

heterogeneous

_____ group.

8. A heterogeneous group usually occurs when no attempt is made to select group members on the

characteristic(s)

basis of some common _____.

9. A *homogeneous* group may be defined as a group consisting of members who have been selected

characteristic(s)

on the basis of some common _____.
A *heterogeneous* group may be defined as a group consisting of members who have *not* been selected on the basis of some common

characteristic(s)

_____.

10. In a group of cattle selected on the basis of the common characteristic of color, the group would

homogeneous

be _____ only in reference to the characteristic of color. Since the cattle probably would be dissimiliar in most other characteristics,

heterogeneous

the group would be called a _____ group in reference to other characteristics.

characteristics

heterogeneous

11. Most groups are homogeneous only in reference to a limited number of common _____. In most other characteristics, the groups probably would be ⊃ _____.

limited

12. When grouping children for instruction, you can place children in groups which are homogeneous, but the groups would be homogeneous only in reference to a _____ number of common characteristics.

purpose

13. Since the first principle of effective grouping is that a purpose for grouping must be established before grouping can take place, any attempt to make groups homogeneous would focus on characteristics related to a specific _____.

14. Some common characteristics, or criteria, which have been used to group children homogeneously for reading instruction are listed below:

reading achievement scores	social maturity
readiness	interest
physical maturity	intelligence
sex	friendship preferences
mental age	personality traits
chronological age	reading skills
	language facility

Even though homogeneous groups could be established on the basis of one or more of these

characteristics

heterogeneous

characteristics

common _____, the groups probably would be _____ on the basis of the remaining _____.

15. Since there are so many characteristics which can be used to group children for instruction, it is advisable that the selection of a characteristic or characteristics to form a basis for grouping be guided by the principle that grouping should always be conducted in relation to a specific

purpose

_____.

16. In a well-managed classroom, it is probable that a teacher of reading would establish a variety of

objectives or purposes in her teaching. As her objectives are met and as the needs of her pupils change, groups also should _____.

change

_____.

17. Since groups are established in relation to a specific purpose, it can be seen that as purposes

change   change, groups should also _____.

18. There should be a change in the structure of groups every time there is a change in the

purpose   _____ for grouping.

19. Another way of stating the preceding premise is to say that effective grouping involves observance of the principle of *flexibility* — a willingness to change the composition of groups whenever the *purpose* for grouping is

changed   _____.

20. Suppose that a teacher has identified as his purpose the teaching of a lesson in reading comprehension. He might look at a list of characteristics on the basis of which homogeneous groups could be established and decide that, for his purpose of teaching a lesson in reading comprehension, the criterion of reading achievement would be

characteristic   an appropriate common _____ to use in grouping his pupils.

21. The teacher would then decide that pupils who have achieved at about the same level in reading

group   would be placed in the same _____.

22. Reading achievement level is usually determined on the basis of a pupil's *average score* on several subtest scores in a standardized test. Pupils usually are not placed in a group on the basis of specific subtest scores, but only the basis of their

average   _____ scores.

23. An example of subtest scores for a boy named Tom might be the following:

Test	Grade Level Score
Vocabulary	4.0
Comprehension	2.0

In Tom's case, his average score, or reading

3.0   achievement level, would be ———————.

24. An example of subtest scores for a girl named Sue might be the following:

Test	Grade Level Score
Vocabulary	2.0
Comprehension	4.0

In Sue's case, her average score, or achievement

3.0   level, would be ———————.

25. In each of the preceding examples, the score

3.0   ——————— was the average score for each pupil. Even though the average scores were the same, however, the scores on the subtests were

different (or not   ———————.
    the same)

26. Different subtest scores could yield the same

average   ——————— score.

27. Assume that the teacher's purpose for grouping the children on the basis of their average reading scores, or achievement, is to provide instruction in reading comprehension. However, since Tom's subtest score was different from Sue's subtest score in comprehension, the needs of these two children for practice in reading comprehen-

different   sion also would be ———————.

28. Since grouping should always be related to a purpose, the use of average reading achievement scores would be inappropriate for an exercise in a specific skill, such as comprehension, because the group would be *homogeneous* only in relation to the group members' average reading scores. In relation to the scores of group members in the subtests, the groups would be

heterogeneous   ———————.

subtest

29. Instead of using "reading achievement," which is the average of the subtest scores and which provides too general an index of ability for effective grouping, the teacher should probably focus on the specific _____ scores.

homogeneous

disadvantages

30. Regardless of which criterion or which combinations of criteria for grouping are used, it is virtually impossible to establish groups which are _____ in all respects. Each criterion for grouping, when examined in relation to a specific purpose, could possess certain advantages and certain _____.

disadvantages

changed

31. While the use of a given criterion for grouping might present advantages in relation to any given purpose, the same criterion, when applied in grouping for a different purpose, might present _____. Therefore, as the purpose for grouping is changed, the criterion or criteria for grouping should also be _____.

Review Questions

1. What is meant by the term *homogeneous group?* (See Frame 5 to check your answer.)

2. What is meant by the term *heterogeneous group?* (See Frame 7 to check your answer.)

3. What is one disadvantage in using average scores on achievement tests as a grouping criterion? (See Frames 26 and 27 to check your answer.)

4. Which two principles should be observed in grouping for instruction? (See Frames 15 and 19 to check your answer.)

Planning for
Instruction in Reading

OBJECTIVE: Given a pencil and paper, upon completion of this lesson, the reader will be able to write a valid behavioral objective.

PART ONE: Writing Behavioral Objectives

1. A behavioral objective has two main elements. One of the main elements is a *situation,* which directly describes or indirectly implies the circumstances in which a learner is placed. In the objective above, the reader can visualize himself with a pencil and a sheet of paper, which is a

situation or
circumstances

direct description of the_____in which the learner is placed.

2. If the objective above would have said, "Given a multiple choice test upon completion of the lesson, the reader will be able to correctly mark all items containing behavioral objectives," the visualization of the reader, a test, and a pencil would also be a direct description of a

situation

_____.

3. In some behavioral objectives, however, there is no direct description of a situation. The behavior required of the learner only *implies* the situation. If the objective at the top of the page had said, "Upon completion of this lesson the reader will be able to write a valid behavioral objective," it would be apparent that the learner would have to have something to write with and something to write on. The behavior of the learner — writ-

situation or
    circumstances

ing — implies the _____ in which the learner finds himself.

4. Similarly, in the objective, "Upon completion of the lesson, the learner will be able to sink a free

implied

throw," the situation is _____. To sink a free throw, the learner would have to be placed in a situation which includes a basketball hoop

basketball

and a _____. The situation in this ob-

behavior

jective is implied by the _____ required of the learner.

5. Inclusion of the behavior of the learner is the second element of a behavioral objective. This second element, the learner's behavior, is called the *response*. In the objective at the beginning of the lesson, the student with a pencil and paper is a description of the situation. What the student does — write — is a description of the

response

_____.

6. The response in a behavioral objective must always be observable or measurable. "Write" would be an appropriate word to use to describe

observable

a response because it is _____. In the objective which states that the learner will be able to mark all items, "mark" would be an appropriate word to use to describe a response be-

observable,
    measurable

cause it is both _____ and _____.

7. In the objective which states that students will sink a free throw, "sink" would be an appropriate word to use to describe a response because it is

observable or
    measurable

_____.

8. In the objective, "Students will become familiar with the planets," however, the words "will become familiar with" would not be appropriate words to use in a behavioral objective because

they describe a response which is not readily

observable,
measurable

_____ or _____.

9. In the objective, "On completion of the lesson, students will know quotations from the New Testament," the word "know" would/would not be an appropriate word because it does/does not describe an observable or measurable response. (Underline the correct answers.)

would not
does not

10. To summarize the preceding frames, it can be said that a behavioral objective has two main elements, a directly described or indirectly

described or
implied

_____ situation, in which a learner finds

observable

himself, and an _____ or measurable

response

_____ which is the behavior required of the learner.

11. To facilitate the task of writing a behavioral objective, it is often desirable to begin the objective with the word "Given," followed by a description of the situation, and then to include the words, "the student will be able to," followed

response

by a description of the _____. The following model illustrates this idea.

Given _____ the student will be
        (situation)
able to _____
            (response)

12. Using the model, the writer of the behavioral objective would be able to write a behavioral objective by merely filling in the blank space

situation

describing the _____ and by filling in a

observable

response which is either _____ or measurable.

13. Return to the objective on page 87 which precedes this lesson. Using the model below, fill in the blank spaces with the appropriate words.

the reader will

be able to

> Given *a pencil and paper* _____
>   *(situation)*
> _____ *write a valid*
> *behavioral objective.*
>   *(response)*

Levels of Performance

1. In the behavioral objective, "Given a pencil and paper, students will be able to list the names of the provinces of Canada," the number of students who will list the names as well as the number of the provinces to be listed is not stated. The word "students," without a quantity or number indicated, implies *all* students. Similarly, "will list the provinces" implies the listing of

all

_____ provinces.

2. The number of students implied or directly specified in a behavioral objective is called the *class quantity index*. Since the objective in the preceding frame implied that all students would be able to do something, *all* students, or *100%* of

quantity

the class, would be the class _____

index

_____, because the portion of the class, or quantity of the class who will be able to do a given thing, is specified.

3. Since it is uncommon that all of a class will be able to perform a specific task, it is usually desirable to specify *how many* students will be able to do a given action. Specifying how many students can perform a given action would be spec-

quantity index

ifying a class _____ _____.

4. In the objective, "Given a basketball and a basketball hoop, 80% of the class will be able to sink a free throw," the class quantity index would

80%

be _____.

5. Similarly, if an objective stated that 30 children out of a class of 35 would be able to do a given action, 30/35, or "30 students" would indicate the

class quantity
  index

_____ _____ _____.

6. It is desirable to specify how many students — the class quantity index — can perform a given behavior, because in the absence of such speci-

100

ficity, the implied quantity of the class is ____% of the students, which would be an unlikely occurrence unless the objective is relatively simple.

7. The model for a behavioral objective can be readily altered to include provision for a class quantity index. The model would look like this:

> Given _____, _____
>   *(situation)*   *(how many?)*
> students will be able to _____
>   *(response)*

In the model, neither the situation nor the response has been changed. The only change is that the number of students who can do the re-

class quantity

sponse, or the _____ _____

index

_____ has been accounted for.

8. Just as it may be unlikely that 100% of the students will be able to perform a given behavior, it is also unlikely that a behavior will be performed with 100% accuracy. As stated earlier in this lesson, the response, "will list the provinces,"

all

implies the listing of _____ provinces,

100

or ____% accuracy.

9. The number of provinces to be listed, or the accuracy level with which the listing is done, is called the *student minimal performance level,* because it tells the expected level of performance for each student. Therefore, any time an objec-

tive specifies the percentage of accuracy that students will attain, or how much each student will

student

do, the objective is specifying a _____ minimal performance level.

10. One hundred percent accuracy in listing provinces on the part of each student in the 80% of the class identified would specify a student min-

100

imal performance level of at least ____% for each student in the 80% of the class.

11. If an objective states that 80% of a class will be able to list all provinces, the number 80% would

class

represent the _____ quantity index, and the words "all provinces" would identify the level of accuracy — how much — each student of the 80% would attain. Therefore, "all prov-

student

inces" would represent the _____ minimal performance level.

12. It is desirable in a behavioral objective to specify a student minimal performance level as well as a class quantity index. Leaving either specifica-

100

tion out implies a performance level of ____%.

13. Therefore, in the objective, "Given 10 problems on a math test, 60% of the class will correctly solve at least six problems," an observer would not expect all children to solve all problems,

class quantity

because both the _____ _____

index, student

_____ and the _____ minimal performance level are directly stated.

14. However, in the objective, "Given a basketball and a basketball hoop, students will be able to sink free throws," an observer could infer that *all* students would sink *all* free throws, because 100% of the students and 100% accuracy are implied, since the student minimal level and class

stated or specified

quantity index are not directly _____ .

15. Since it is desirable to include student minimal levels and a class quantity index, as well as a

situation

_____ and an observable or measurable

response

_____, the model for a behavioral objective can be further altered to include a provision for the student minimal level. The final form of the model would look like the following:

> Given_____ _____
>   *(situation)*   (how many?)
>   (class quantity
>   index)
>
> students will be able to_____
>   (how much, or per-
>   centage of accuracy)
> _____.
>   *(response)*

16. Even though a statement of an objective might include a situation, a response, a class quantity index, and a student minimal performance level, to be called an *objective,* the student must focus on the desired response of the learner *after* he receives instruction — that is, on the outcome of

instruction

instruction — not on the _____ itself.

17. For example, even though the statement "Given cards and markers, all students will play a game of sight word Bingo" contains a situation, a response, and a class quantity index, and although a student minimal performance level is implied, the statement does not focus on the *outcome* of instruction, but it focuses, instead, on the

instruction

_____.

18. If a statement focuses on an instructional activity, rather than on the outcome or goal of instruction, the statement could not necessarily be called a

objective

behavioral _____.

19. To call a statement an objective, it would be necessary to determine whether the behaviors,

	or responses, are a part of instruction, or whether
outcomes or goals	they are the intended _____ of the instruction.
	20. The statement "Four out of five players will be able to play a quarter of basketball, using the backboard on all lay-up shots," might be a description of an activity if the behavior is a part of instruction, or it might be a behavioral objective
outcome or goal	if the behavior is the intended _____ of instruction.
	21. A behavioral objective has as its focus the
outcome or goal	_____ of instruction, not the activities of the learner which take place as a part of the
instruction	_____.

Review Exercise

1. Using the form suggested in the model, write a behavioral objective which includes both a student minimal performance level and a class quantity index, and which focuses on the outcome of instruction.

PART TWO: The Directed Reading Lesson (DRL)

OBJECTIVE: The reader will be able to list and describe the steps followed in conducting a directed reading lesson.

	1. One type of instruction which is common to classrooms in which reading is taught is instruction in reading skills which takes place through the use of a short story or a short expository selection. Instead of allowing pupils to read independently, without direction, the teacher directs the pupils' reading so that specific skill development objectives can be achieved. Since the teacher directs the pupils' reading, this type
directed	of lesson is called a _____ reading lesson.
	2. In a directed reading lesson, knowing that a selection is merely a vehicle for teaching skills,

the teacher follows a series of steps to achieve the specific objectives he has in mind. If a series of steps is followed to achieve specific objectives, it is logical to assume that the first step in the series of steps in a directed reading lesson is to

objectives

state the specific _____ of the lesson.

3. Once the objectives have been stated, the first problem facing the teacher is to motivate the reader to read the selection. Since most stories and illustrations in basal readers have been selected, in part, because they are of interest to children, step two in a directed reading lesson,

motivating

_____ the reader to read the selection, is usually not a difficult or time-consuming step.

4. In most stories, story titles and illustrations are chosen, in part, to stimulate pupils' interest. Therefore, one way a teacher can carry out step two is to discuss what the story might be about,

title

based on information provided by the _____

illustrations

of the story or by the _____ which accompany the story.

5. Frequently, stories are about events that are similar to experiences the pupils have had. A teacher can often motivate pupils by asking them "experience" questions. For example, if a story title is "Rattlesnake Cave," the teacher can ask, "Has anyone in class ever been frightened by a rattlesnake?" Experience questions can motivate even reluctant pupils, because few people have difficulty talking about their own interesting

experiences

_____.

6. Once motivation has been stimulated by a dis-

illustrations

cussion of the title or _____, or by a

experiences

discussion of personal _____ similar to the experiences suggested by the title or illustrations, the teacher can proceed from step two —

directed

motivation — to step three in a _____

reading lesson

_____ _____.

7. Step three of a directed reading lesson is not necessary if pupils can readily answer experience questions provided in step two, since in step three the teacher is concerned with *building a background* of experiences for understanding the story. If, though, pupil responses indicate that they have not had many of the experiences anticipated in the story, it is necessary for the teacher

build, background

to _____ a _____ of experiences for understanding the story.

8. The amount of effort a teacher will have to expend in building a background can be readily determined by examining the story and by "examining" the pupil. For example, if an inner-city child is exposed to a story about ranch life in Wyoming which includes obscure terms, such as "line camp" and "BLM lands," there will probably be a big conceptual gap between the pupil's experiences and experiences in the story, so the

building, background

step of _____ a _____ for understanding will require careful planning.

9. Suppose, though, that an inner-city child is exposed to a story about life in the inner city. In this case, the teacher would not have to be too concerned about building a background because an examination of the story and of the learner indicates that the anticipated experiences of story characters and the experiences of the learner will be similar. The learner will have a sufficient back-

experience(s)

ground of _____ to adequately understand the story.

10. The step of building a background usually requires that the teacher merely provide information for the pupils to help them more fully understand or appreciate a story. For instance, in the story *David and Goliath*, if the teacher merely explains that David was an adolescent and that Goliath was a warrior almost ten feet tall, and compares ten feet to the height of a basketball hoop, the background-building would be brief and simple, but it would contribute greatly to

understanding,
appreciation

the pupils' _____ and _____ of the story.

objective

11. After stating a specific _____, discussing the title, illustrations, and pupils' experiences, or providing other motivation for the reader to

building

read the story, as well as _____ a

background

_____ for understanding and appreciating the story, the teacher can carry out a

directed, reading

fourth step in a _____ _____

lesson

_____.

12. The fourth step in conducting a directed reading lesson is *introducing new words* used in the selection. "New words" may be words which are completely unfamiliar to the pupils, or they may be words which are unfamiliar only in print. In either case, if the pupil is to fully understand the selection, it is sometimes necessary for the

introduce

teacher to _____ the new words.

13. Because the pupil may have reached quite an advanced stage in his ability to independently use *word attack skills,* the teacher may need to do little to introduce the new words. The amount of ability pupils possess in using word attack skills will determine to what extent the teacher

introduce, new

will need to _____ the _____ words.

14. Whether a word is *unfamiliar* both in its spoken form and its printed form, or whether it is *familiar* in its spoken form and *unfamiliar* only in

printed

its _____ form will also determine whether the teacher will need to introduce the new words.

15. Since the use of context clues is both a word attack skill and a comprehension skill — that is, it suggests what an unfamiliar word might *be* as well as what it might *mean* — it is usually desirable for the teacher to introduce selected words

context

clues

in context, so that the pupil can use _____

_____ to decode or comprehend the new words.

16. If the contexts in which new words are found in the story strongly suggest what the new words are or what they mean, or if pupils possess advanced dictionary skills to help them determine pronunciation and meaning, it is desirable for

introduce new

words

the teacher *not* to _____ _____

_____.

17. Thus, the fourth step in a directed reading lesson, *introducing new words,* is an optional step because it may be *desirable* to introduce new words if the pupils possess limited word attack skills or if the contexts in which new words are found are weak, or it may be *undesirable* to introduce new words if pupils possess adequate

word attack

contexts

_____ _____ skills and if the

_____ in which new words are found are suggestive of both the pronunciation and the

meaning

_____ of the new words.

18. Suppose that a teacher has carried out the first four steps of a directed reading lesson:

objectives

Step one, *stating specific* _____ for instruction;

motivating

Step two, _____ the pupil to read;

building, background

Step three, _____ a _____ for understanding; and the optional step,

introducing new

Step four, _____ _____

words

_____, it is then desirable to carry out another optional step, that of *providing purposes for reading.*

19. Providing purposes for reading is a desirable step to follow because, just as it would be likely that

there would be much unproductive effort on the part of a teacher who did not have a specific

objective

_____ or purpose in mind in providing instruction, it would also be likely that there would be much unproductive effort on the part

purpose

of a pupil who did not have a _____ in mind for reading a selection.

20. A purpose for reading has been demonstrated to be very helpful to a reader in comprehending what is read. For a beginning reader, the teacher usually attempts to help the pupils comprehend what is read not only through building a background and introducing new words, but also by providing a purpose for reading. As a pupil matures in his ability to read, however, it is desirable to teach him to provide his own

purpose

_____ for reading a selection.

21. The step of providing purposes for reading is optional, also, because a teacher would provide the purpose only if he had a specific objective in

provide

mind or if the reader could not _____

purpose(s)

his own _____ for reading the selection.

22. In providing purposes for reading, a teacher can partially individualize instruction by providing challenging purposes for high-achieving readers, and less challenging purposes for low-achieving readers. In other words, the reading ability of each pupil helps the teacher decide what kind of purpose to provide for each student. By providing different purposes for different pupils a

individualize

teacher can _____ instruction to some extent.

23. The amount of effort or time expended on each step in a directed reading lesson would depend partially upon the reading ability level of the pupils. In one sense, therefore, not only are the steps of introducing new words and providing purposes optional, but with the exception of the

objective

optional

purposes

silent

silent

motivation, building

background,
    introducing
words

discussion

first step of *stating a specific* _____,
every step in a directed reading lesson is

_____, depending on the ability level
of the pupils and the specific objective of the
teacher.

24. Following the steps taken by the teacher in preparing the pupils to read, the selection is read
silently by the pupils, so that each student can
proceed at his own pace, apply his ability in the
word attack skills, and read to achieve the

_____ provided by the teacher or the
purposes he, himself, provided.

25. Thus, the sixth step in a directed reading lesson

is _____ reading of the story by the
pupils.

26. In order for the teacher to determine whether
his specific objectives were partially met, and
whether students achieved the purposes for
reading, a seventh step in a directed reading
lesson is carried out. The seventh step is a *discussion* of what the students learned through

carrying out their _____ reading of the
selection.

27. The discussion also helps the teacher determine
whether an adequate job was done in the first
steps of the directed reading lesson, namely,

_____ of the reader, _____ a

_____, and _____

new _____.

28. An observant teacher can also determine the degree of comprehension of the story by carefully

following the nature of the _____ carried out by the pupils.

29. The discussion of a story might lead into and
include another optional step in a directed read-

ing lesson—oral reading. For example, if a question arises in the discussion, the teacher may use

oral

_____ reading of a particular section of the story to prove or disprove a point raised in

discussion

the _____.

30. Oral reading of parts of a story, besides providing evidence for points raised in the discussion, can also be used for diagnosis, for sharing, for teaching reading with appropriate intonation, or for pleasure. If it is used to teach appropriate intonation, then only those sections of the story which offer opportunities to practice varied intonation should be used, since all parts of a story are not equally suited to the practice of devel-

intonation

oping reading with appropriate _____.

31. Similarly, all parts of a story, or the whole story, would not be equally suited to prove or disprove

discussion

points which arise in the _____ which

silent

follows pupils' _____ reading.

32. Further, if a teacher wanted to diagnose mastery of new words, oral reading of only those sections containing the new words would be used, since all parts of the story—every paragraph—would

new words

not likely include _____ _____.

33. Since for any given purpose it is not necessary or desirable to read the total story orally, it is logical to assume that seldom should oral reading of the

whole or total
story

_____ _____ occur.

34. Just as instruction in a directed reading lesson is conducted with a purpose, and silent reading of a story is conducted with a purpose, so also should oral reading of a story be conducted with

purpose

a _____.

35. It can therefore be concluded that "barber shop" oral reading—where each pupil awaits his turn

to orally read a paragraph in sequence, just as each customer awaits his turn for a haircut in a barber shop — is rarely justifiable, because it is usually oral reading which is conducted without

purpose   a specific _____ .

36. Simply stated, in conducting the step of oral reading in a directed reading lesson, a teacher can be guided by the principle that *what* is read orally and *who* should read orally depend on the

purpose   _____ for which oral reading is used.

37. A final step in a directed reading lesson is to reinforce or *teach the skills* specified in the objective for the directed reading lesson, in the event that the skills have not been taught in

introducing   the steps of _____ new words, provid-

purposes   ing _____ for reading, conducting a

discussion   _____ following silent reading, or car-

oral   rying on purposeful _____ reading.

38. If a teacher desires to teach skills effectively through a story it is necessary that the reader be sufficiently motivated to read the story, that he have sufficient background to understand the story, and that he possess the ability to master new words in the story. If one of the teacher's specific objectives is to enhance comprehension, it is also necessary for the learner to read silently with a purpose so that he can adequately participate in a discussion, backing up his opinions, if necessary, with appropriate oral reading. It is for these reasons that a teacher follows these steps:

specific objective   Step one: stating a _____ _____ ;

motivating   Step two: creating interest, or _____ children for reading;

background   Step three: building a _____ for understanding;

introducing new	Step four: _____ _____
words	_____;
purposes	Step five: providing _____ for reading;
silent	Step six: allowing time for _____ reading by the pupil;
discussion	Step seven: conducting a _____ following silent reading; and
oral	Step eight: conducting purposeful _____ reading of parts of the selection, in addition to teaching skills, in carrying out a successful
directed reading lesson	_____ _____ _____.

PART THREE: Teaching a Reading Skill

OBJECTIVE: The reader will be able to list and describe several steps which can be followed in teaching a reading skill.

1. At the time a learner is receiving initial instruction in a reading skill, it is helpful to be guided by certain criteria in designing a lesson. Each criterion will help to focus the attention of the learner on the reading _____ to be learned.

skill

2. One concern in setting up a skills lesson is the *choice of printed material* to be used with the learner. The material should not present reading difficulties for the learner other than that of the specific skill to be introduced. Under this condition, most difficulties in learning the skill will be removed, permitting the focus of attention to be on the skill to be _____.

learned

3. An example of the above condition is the following: Suppose that the words *action* and *mention* are selected to introduce the sound-symbol relationship for the common ending *-tion*. These words are familiar to the learner in both pronunciation and meaning. Therefore, attention can

-tion

be focused on the ending of each of these words, which have been especially selected to teach the sound-symbol relationship of the common ending ——————.

-tion

4. Suppose, though, that the words *ostentation* and *oscillation* are selected to teach the common ending -*tion*. These words would be inappropriate material for teaching the common ending -*tion* because the learner would be confronted with an unfamiliar word as well as with the unfamiliar ending ——————.

appropriate

5. The examples above illustrate that material chosen for teaching a skill can be appropriate or inappropriate. Material which confronts the learner with a variety of unfamiliar concepts would be inappropriate for teaching a specific reading skill. Material which confronts the learner with only one unfamiliar concept—that of the skill to be learned—would be ——————— for teaching a specific reading skill.

material

one

6. It is apparent then that one criterion which can guide a teacher in teaching a reading skill is that the printed ——————— chosen to teach the skill should present the child with only ——————— unfamiliar concept—that of the skill to be learned.

learned

7. Learning is enhanced if the learner knows precisely the reading skill he is to learn in any given lesson. A second criterion of a skill lesson is the early *identification of the* specific reading *skill* to be ——————.

importance

8. In introducing a new reading skill, the teacher should *reveal the importance of the skill* to the reader. A skill will be accepted as necessary if the learner senses its ——————— for him.

9. Suppose, for example, that a teacher says to a child, "You will probably never use the skill I want to teach you today, but since it is included

in your book, I'd like you to learn it anyway." It is probable that the learner will have little interest in learning the skill, since the teacher has, in effect, led the learner to conclude that

important the skill is not ——————— to him.

10. On the other hand, suppose that a teacher convinces a child that a new skill to be learned is of great importance to him in becoming an effective reader. In this case, the child would be more likely to want to learn the skill, since the teacher

important has convinced him that the skill is ———————
to him in reaching his goal of becoming an effective reader.

11. The desirability of identifying a skill and revealing its importance to the learner is a second

criterion ——————— which can guide the teacher in teaching a reading skill.

12. Besides selecting appropriate material and identifying the skill and its importance, the introductory lesson should *provide an illustration of the use of the skill* in a situation the learner can comprehend. The purpose of providing an

illustration ——————— of the correct use of the skill is to further the learner's understanding of the skill.

13. The desirability of illustrating the use of a skill in a situation the learner can understand is a

criterion third ——————— which can guide a teacher in teaching a reading skill.

14. Yet another criterion of an effective skill lesson is the provision made for *checking on the developing understanding* the learner has of the new skill. A discussion of the illustration in which the skill is used, for example, will enable the teacher

check to ——————— on the developing understanding the learner is gaining about the skill.

15. At this point, a teacher would have four criteria to guide him in teaching a reading skill. The first criterion would be that the material selected

one

skill

for teaching a skill confront the learner with only
_____ unfamiliar concept—that of the
_____ to be learned.

16. The second criterion would be that the teacher
    identify the skill and reveal its _____
    to the learner.

importance

17. The third and fourth criteria would be that the
    teacher illustrate the use of the _____
    in a situation the learner can comprehend and
    that the teacher _____ on the develop-
    ing understanding the learner is gaining about
    the skill.

skill

check

18. During the introductory lesson, the learner
    should have an opportunity for *initial practice* of
    the skill in an atmosphere *free of threat*. Here,
    the teacher is in a position to give immediate
    reinforcement to responses the learner gives in
    this initial _____ exercise.

practice

19. The fifth and sixth criteria which can guide a
    teacher in teaching a reading skill would be that
    the learner have an opportunity for initial
    _____ of the skill during the introduc-
    tory lesson and that the learner's practice take
    place in an atmosphere free of _____.

practice

threat

20. A final criterion which can guide a teacher in
    teaching a reading skill is that a *discussion should
    follow* an initial *practice* experience in order to
    clear up immediately any misunderstanding the
    learner still has about the new skill. The give-and-
    take that is carried on among learners and the
    teacher tends to clarify misunderstandings and
    points up the value of providing for such
    _____ in a lesson.

discussion

21. In a lesson introducing a new reading skill, the
    learner should be able to sense that the lesson
    is set up for his benefit. Each activity in the les-
    son should be designed to bring about a more

skill

thorough understanding of the _____ on the part of the learner.

22. In summarizing the components of an effective reading skill lesson, it is well to keep the following in mind:

    a. The difficulty of the material for the learner should focus only on the specific

skill

    _____ to be learned.

    b. The skill to be learned should be clearly

identified

    _____.

    c. The importance of the skill should be

learner

    sensed by the _____.

    d. The correct use of the skill should be

illustrated

    _____ in the lesson to show its application.

    e. A check should be made often through discussion to determine the degree to which

understands

    the learner _____ the skill.

    f. The lesson should provide the learner with

practice

    an opportunity to get initial _____ in the use of the skill.

Review Questions

1. Recall the four major activities carried out by a teacher in teaching a story unit. (See Frames 32-36 of Part One to check your answer.)

2. List the criteria of a well-planned lesson for teaching a reading skill. (See Frames 22-27 of Part Two to check your answer.)

Approaches to Beginning Reading

OBJECTIVE: The reader will be able to describe the components, advantages, and limitations of a basal reading series.

PART ONE: What Is a Basal Reading Series?

read

1. An essential component of any basal reading series is a set of books, commonly called *readers*. The books are called *readers* because they provide selections to be used as vehicles through which children will receive instruction in learning how to ———————.

anthology

2. Each book, or *reader,* in a basal reading series is usually an *anthology,* which often includes short stories, articles, poems, plays, puzzles, jokes, anecdotes, and, in some cases, skill-building exercises. Although every anthology is not a reader in a basal reading series, almost every reader in a basal reading series is an ———————.

read

3. Each reader, or anthology, in a basal reading series has been carefully graded according to readability. *Carefully graded according to readability* means that selections in each reader have been chosen, in part, on the basis of how difficult they are for children to ———————.

4. An example of how readers have been graded, or divided into levels in a basal reading series, might be the following:

Reading Readiness Book
First Preprimer
Second Preprimer
Third Preprimer
Primer (Level One, First Book) (1-1)

Level One, Second Book	(1-2)
Level Two, First Book	(2-1)
Level Two, Second Book	(2-2)
Level Three, First Book	(3-1)
Level Three, Second Book	(3-2)
Level Four	(4)
Level Five	(5)
Level Six, etc.	(6)

The book designed to be used first would be the Reading Readiness Book. The book designed to be used last in a series in which only six levels are provided would be the Level _____ book.

Six

5. The book designed to be used immediately before using the (3-2) book would be the _____ book.

(3-1)

6. In recent publications of basal reading series, letters have been used instead of numbers to designate levels of difficulty. In schools, such as *open concept* schools, in which numbers are not used to designate grade placement of children, basal series in which _____ designate the levels of difficulty of the basal readers are often used.

letters

7. With each book in a basal reading series, a *workbook* is commonly provided. The workbook contains practice exercises correlated with skills introduced in the readers. For example, a child might be introduced to a skill in his reader and then provided with an opportunity for further practice in the skill in the _____.

workbook

8. Besides providing a systematic skill development program in the books and workbooks written for children, a basal reading series also provides a teacher's manual which includes suggestions for *teaching* reading. The manual is designed to be used by the _____.

teacher

9. The directions for teaching reading that are found in the teacher's manual include suggestions for the teacher in teaching new vocabulary, specific

word attack skills, and specific comprehension skills, as well as suggestions for developing appreciation for reading. Therefore, if a specific reading skill is introduced in a child's reader, suggestions for teaching the skill can be found in

teacher's manual

the _____ _____.

10. In addition to the readers, workbooks, and teacher's manual, a basal reading series might also include other teaching-learning aids, such as supplementary reading materials or lists of materials, filmstrips, records, worksheet masters, and other aids. Suggestions regarding the appropriate use

teacher's manual

of these aids can be found in the _____

_____.

11. The supplementary materials in a basal reading series are included to help teachers provide for individual differences among children. In response to the needs of individual children, a teacher can select different supplementary mate-

children or pupils

rials for different _____.

12. Since children differ in their needs for various reading skills, besides selecting different supplementary materals for different children, a teacher can select different workbook exercises for dif-

children

ferent _____.

13. It is also important to remember that each teacher is also different in many ways from every other teacher. Therefore, it is not likely that all teachers would want to attempt to use every

teacher's

teaching suggestion provided in the _____

manual

_____.

14. There are several advantages to using a basal reading series, especially for beginning teachers. Since many beginning teachers lack the experience which might make them confident in planning for instruction, the suggestions in the teacher's manual can be of great help to them. Well-planned teacher's manuals, then, can be

advantage

regarded as an _____ of a basal reading series.

15. Beginning teachers are also frequently concerned about the sequence or selection of reading skills to be taught. Since a basal reading series presents a systematic skill development program which is grounded in research and a thoroughly developed philosophy of teaching reading, a beginning teacher can have confidence in the appropriateness of the scope and sequence of reading skills presented in a basal series. A systematic skill development program grounded in research and a thoroughly developed philosophy

advantage

can be cited as an additional _____ of a basal reading series.

16. Limitations of a basal reading series are usually encountered when a basal series is misused. For example, misuse is evident when all children in a class are required to read the same material, or when teachers are reluctant to adapt the suggestions in the teacher's manual to their unique teaching situations. A limitation encountered when a basal series is misused, then, occurs when teachers fail to recognize that children and teach-

different

ers are different and that they have _____ needs.

17. Another frequently encountered misuse of a basal reading series which imposes a limitation on the effectiveness of such series occurs when teachers use a basal reading series as a *total* reading program. Although a basal reading series is a comprehensive program which provides a systematic teaching-learning plan, it is not advisable to use

total

a basal series as a _____ reading program.

18. In summary, a basal reading series is a set of

readers

graded books, commonly called _____.

anthology

Each reader is an _____ of a variety of reading material. Accompanying each book is a

workbook

_____ which can be used to furnish practice in specific reading skills. Suggestions for

teacher's

the teacher can be found in the _____

manual

_____. The suggestions in the teacher's

manual include not only recommendations for teaching, but also suggestions for using supple-

materials

mentary _____ which may be provided with the basal series. The major objective of a basal reading series is the providing of a system-

skill

atic _____ development program in reading.

Review Questions

1. What are the components of a basal reading series? (See Frames 1, 7, 8, and 10 to check your answer.)

2. Identify two advantages which a basal reading series might provide for a beginning teacher. (See Frames 14 and 15 to check your answer.)

3. Limitations in the effectiveness of a basal reading series can occur when a basal reading series is misused. In what ways are basal reading series commonly misused? (See Frames 16 and 17 to check your answer.)

PART TWO: Augmented Alphabets—The Initial Teaching Alphabet (i/t/a)

OBJECTIVE: The reader will be able to define the term *augmented alphabets,* and describe the use of the i/t/a in an approach to teaching reading. The reader will be able to state the advantages and disadvantages of augmented alphabet approaches.

1. An earlier lesson in this book discussed the necessity of teaching beginning readers the concept of letter-sound association, which means, simply, that individual letters and groups of letters stand

sounds

for _____.

2. In mastering the learning of letters, letter combinations, and the sounds they represent, one problem every beginning reader of English encounters is that different letters and letter com-

sounds

binations often represent the same _____.

3. For example, the words listed in the box to the right might pose a problem to a beginning reader, because, although the *letters* in the word endings are *different,* the sounds in the word endings are the

by
buy
h*igh*
d*ie*

same   _____.

4. Another way of expressing the idea that different letters often have the same sound would be to say that the sound-symbol relationship is not *consistent.* Thus, in the words *meet* and *seat,* since different letters represent the same vowel

sound   _____, it could be said that the sound-

consistent   symbol relationship is not _____.

5. Besides the fact that different letters can represent the same sounds, the words in the box to the right show that different sounds can be represented by the same

th*rough*
th*ough*
rough

letters   _____.

6. When different *sounds* are represented by the same letters, the sound-symbol relationship is not

th*rough*
rough

consistent   _____. The sound-symbol relationship is also not consistent when different *letters* represent the

b*uy*
h*igh*

sound   same _____.

7. One way to overcome the problem of sound-symbol relationships which are not consistent would be to spell words in a way that would always represent a given sound by the same

letter(s)   _____. This would, in turn, ensure that a given letter or letters would represent the same

sound   _____.

8. If the same letter or letters would consistently represent the same sound, the sound-symbol relationship would be

consistent   lationship would be _____.

9. Our traditional English alphabet, or *traditional orthography* as it is sometimes called, does not

sound-symbol
  relationship

have enough letters to ensure a consistent

_____-_____ _____
each time a word is written. Therefore, if a consistent sound-symbol relationship is to be provided, additional symbols must also be

provided

_____.

10. When additional symbols are added to the alphabet, or when other additions are made to the alphabet, the alphabet is called an *augmented alphabet.* For example, an alphabet to which different colors have been added so that letters of a given color would always represent a given

augmented

sound would be called an _____ alphabet, because the element of color has been added to it.

11. Similarly, if special marks or symbols were to be added to an alphabet, it could be said that the additional marks or symbols result in an

augmented

_____ alphabet.

12. Many acceptable augmented alphabets have been used successfully in teaching reading. The augmented alphabet presented in this program will serve as an example of an attempt to overcome the problem of a lack of a consistent

relationship

sound-symbol _____ in our traditional orthography.

13. In the *Initial Teaching Alphabet,* or *i/t/a,* additional symbols have been provided to ensure a

sound-symbol
relationship

consistent _____-_____
_____ each time a word is written. Thus, the spelling of the words *by, high, die,* and *buy* would be changed so that the vowel sound

symbol or letter

would be represented by the same _____.

14. In the Initial Teaching Alphabet, the spelling of the words *meat* and *feet,* for example, would also

changed

be _____ so that the sound-symbol relationship would be consistent.

sound

15. The Initial Teaching Alphabet consists of forty-four sound-symbols, each of which always represents the same _____ each time a word is written.

16. Only twenty-four of the letters in our traditional alphabet, or traditional orthography (t.o.), have been included in the Initial Teaching Alphabet; therefore, twenty additional symbols have been added to the Initial Teaching Alphabet to pro-

forty-four

vide the total of _____ sound-symbols.

17. In i/t/a, the *th* sound in the word *this* is represented by the symbol **ſh** . Therefore, the word

ſhis

this would be written _____. The *th* sound in the word *these* would also be written

ſh
sound

_____ since the *th* in *this* and the *th* in *these* have the same _____.

18. In the word *with*, however, the *th* sound would *not* be written with the symbol **ſh** , because in the words *this* and *with*, the letters *th* do not

sound

stand for the same _____.

19. In the Initial Teaching Alphabet, each time a different sound is represented, it is represented with

symbol or letter

a different _____.

20. The Initial Teaching Alphabet has been reproduced on the following page. Following the concept of a consistent sound-symbol relationship,

iglω
canω

write the words *igloo* and *canoe*. _____
_____

21. Remembering that the sound-symbol relationship is consistent only in i/t/a, write the following words in traditional orthography: *ruf, stuf.*

rough, stuff

_____ _____.

22. Since the Initial Teaching Alphabet provides a consistent sound-symbol relationship in beginning reading, both reading *and* writing can be

facilitated. Once a child learns the symbols and the sounds they represent, he can not only read without excessive difficulty, but it is also probable that he will be able to _____ without excessive difficulty.

write

23. Although reading and writing can be facilitated in beginning reading with i/t/a, children eventually must learn how to read in t.o., since most reading materials are written in the conventional alphabet, or traditional _____.

orthography

24. For most children, the change, or transition, from i/t/a to t.o. does not present major problems.

The Initial Teaching Alphabet

Nevertheless, the transition from i/t/a to t.o. can be an additional problem in teaching reading which, although not of concern to the teacher using t.o. materials, is always of concern to the

i/t/a

teacher using _____ materials.

25. Just as the exclusive use of a basal reading series as a total reading program might constitute a limitation in achieving effective teaching and learning of reading, the exclusive use of i/t/a as a total reading program might constitute a limitation on effective teaching and learning of reading. However, while there is an abundance of supplementary reading material written in t.o. available to the teacher using t.o. materials, there are far fewer supplementary materials written in

i/t/a

i/t/a available to the teacher using _____ materials.

26. The most readily apparent potential limitations of i/t/a as a medium in teaching beginning reading are that i/t/a-taught children must make a

t.o. or traditional orthography

transition from i/t/a to _____ and that there is not an abundance of supplementary reading material available to the teacher using the

i/t/a

medium of _____.

27. The most readily apparent advantage of i/t/a materials in teaching beginning reading is that the problem of a lack of a consistent sound-symbol relationship encountered in materials printed in t.o. is not encountered in materials printed in i/t/a. The forty-four sound-symbols of i/t/a assure the beginning reader of always find-

sound-symbol relationship

ing a consistent _____-_____

_____ in his i/t/a reading material.

28. It can be seen then that the most readily apparent advantage of augmented alphabets is that they can be of help in overcoming the problem of a

sound-symbol relationship

lack of a consistent _____-_____

_____ in our traditional orthography. The most readily apparent disadvantages of augmented alphabets are that children must even-

transition

material

| | tually make a _____ to materials which are written in t.o. and that there is not an abun-dance of supplementary reading _____ available which is written with augmented alphabets. |

Review Questions

1. What is meant by the term "augmented alphabet"? (See Frame 10 to check your answer.)

2. How many sound-symbols are used in i/t/a? (See Frame 16 to check your answer.)

3. For which problem in teaching reading are augmented alphabets suggested as a solution? (See Frame 2 to check your answer.)

PART THREE: Programmed Instruction and Programmed Reading

OBJECTIVE: The reader will be able to state the characteristics of programmed materials and describe what is meant by "linear" programs and "intrinsic" programs. The reader will be able to state the advantages and the limitations of programmed materials.

step

frame

response

1. One characteristic of programmed instruction is that it breaks learning into *small steps*. The information being presented to you in this paragraph is an example of a small _____.

2. Each small step is presented in a paragraph. A small step such as the one in this paragraph is called a *frame*. You are now reading information in the second small step or _____.

3. The information in each frame is called the *stimulus*. The answer for each frame is called the *response*. In this frame, you have been given a stimulus. It is now up to you to provide the _____.

4. Each time you check your response, your learning is immediately reinforced. Since you probably

have provided correct responses in most of the preceding frames, the *reinforcement* has been both *immediate and positive.* If your response to the stimulus in this frame is a correct response, the reinforcement will be both immediate and

positive

_____.

5. You have now learned two characteristics of programmed instruction. The first characteristic is

steps

that learning is broken into small _____.
The second characteristic is that programmed in-

positive

struction provides immediate and _____ reinforcement each time a correct response is made.

6. As you proceeded from one frame to another, each stimulus and response provide you with additional information. You have been moving from the "known" to the "unknown." *Moving from the "known" to the "unknown"* is a third characteris-

instruction

tic of programmed _____.

7. In moving from the "known" to the "unknown," you proceeded at your own rate. Because you proceeded at your own rate, this program is an *individualized* program for you. A fourth characteristic of programmed instruction, then, is that

individualized

it is _____ in relation to a learner's rate of learning.

8. When you read the first frame, the stimulus was simple and the response was simple. As you proceeded, however, each stimulus and each reponse became more complex. You have been moving from the simple to the complex. *Moving from the simple to the complex is a fifth*

characteristic

_____ of programmed instruction.

9. These five characteristics are usually found in programmed materials. However, frames which must be followed in sequence without offering the learner an opportunity to skip frames are used only in *linear* programs. Since the frames used in this programmed lesson must be followed in sequence and since no opportunity to skip frames

linear

has been provided, this program is a _____ program.

10. Another type of programmed instruction is the *intrinsic* program, sometimes called a "branching" program. An intrinsic program presents a stimulus and several plausible responses, only

response

one of which is the correct _____.

If you selected "a," go back to frame 10 and review the information presented. Then try Frame 12.

If you selected "b," you are correct. Proceed to Frame 13.

If you selected "c," follow the procedure outlined in "a" above.

11. Several plausible responses have be provided below. Only one response is correct. Although this type of item might possibly be found in a linear program, it would be more likely that it would be found in (mark a, b, or c):

   a. several frames in a row
   b. an intrinsic program
   c. all linear programs

12. Now that you have reviewed Frame 10, you can see why response "b" was the correct response. Response "b" was the correct response for Frame 11 because Frame 11 provided several plausible responses, and one characteristic of intrinsic programs is that they provide several plausible

responses

_____.

13. If you completed Item 11 correctly, you did not have to move backward to Item 10 again or do Item 12 as you would have had to do if you had chosen responses "a" or "c." Therefore, you have progressed more rapidly than a person who might have chosen response "a" or "c" in Item 11. It can be seen then that intrinsic programs

each or every

do not require the learner to complete _____ frame.

14. It can also be seen that although *linear* programs are designed to allow the learner to proceed *forward* only, *intrinsic* programs are designed to

backward

allow the learner to go forward or _____ if a review of a concept is needed.

15. The concepts presented in this book have been presented in the form of a *linear* program. Therefore, although you may have chosen to look back and review certain concepts, the lessons have been designed to allow you to proceed

forward

_____ only while you are actually working through the material.

16. As you proceeded forward, you worked through material which was presented in small steps which

frames

are often called _____. In each frame you were provided with a stimulus; however, you

response(s)

provided the _____. Each time you checked your response and found that it was a correct response, you were provided with reinforcement which was both immediate and

positive

_____.

17. Throughout the programmed lessons, you also

unknown

moved from the "known" to the _____

complex

and from the simple to the _____.

18. The principles of programmed instruction reviewed above have been applied successfully to the teaching of reading, most commonly through the use of linear programs. In programmed reading, therefore, the learner proceeds from the

unknown

known to the _____ and from the sim-

complex

ple to the _____, usually in small steps.

19. Programmed instruction, it should be remembered, also provides immediate and positive reinforcement. In programmed reading, each time a correct response is made in each small step, the learner receives immediate and positive

reinforcement

_____.

20. An apparent advantage of programmed reading is that it is individualized to an extent, since each

child moves through the program at his own

rate or speed   _____.

21. Although linear reading programs provide for
different learning *rates*, every child must still proceed through every concept in every frame in
every programmed reading lesson. Different children not only have different learning *rates*, they
also have different learning *needs*. An apparent
disadvantage of linear reading programs is that
although provision is made for different learning
rates, unless a teacher provides careful instruction, little provision is made for different learning

needs   _____.

Review Questions

1. List several characteristics of programmed instruction. (See Frames
1-8 to check your answer.)

2. What is the difference between a linear program and an intrinsic
program? (See Frames 13 and 14 to check your answer.)

3. What is an apparent advantage in using programmed instruction
to teach reading? What is an apparent disadvantage? (See Frames
20 and 21 to check your answer.)

PART FOUR: The Language Experience Approach

OBJECTIVE: The reader will be able to describe the philosophy of
the language experience approach, to delineate how a
language experience approach might be initiated, and
to state the advantages and limitations of the language
experience approach.

1. A basic principle of language is that thoughts
can be expressed in spoken words. Another way
of stating this principle is that anything an indi-

talk   vidual can think about, he can _____
about.

2. The preceding principle constitutes a basic prem-

child

ise of the *Language Experience Approach* in the teaching of reading. Since beginning reading instruction is usually taught to children in the language they speak, the principle is restated as follows in the Language Experience Approach:

"Anything a _____ can think about, he can talk about."

3. Anything "talked about" or spoken can also be expressed in written form. A second premise of the Language Experience Approach is that anything which can be expressed in oral language

written

can also be expressed in _____ language.

4. Another way of stating the aforementioned premise would be to say that anything a child can say,

write

he can _____.

5. A third premise of the Language Experience Approach is that what is written can be read or, simply, that anything a child can write for himself or anything that others can write for him, he

read

can _____.

6. The three basic premises underlying the Language Experience Approach, then, might be stated as follows:

talk

What a child can think about, he can _____ *about.*

written

What a child can say can be _____.

What a child can write, or what others can write

read

for him, he can _____.

7. Since the first premise of the Language Experience Approach pertains to the child's use of oral language, it can be expected that the initial emphasis in beginning reading instruction in the Language Experience Approach would involve

oral

the use of _____ language.

8. Oral language development is enhanced through developing the skills of listening and speaking.

Therefore, in the initial stages of reading instruction with the Language Experience Approach, much opportunity is provided for the development of the skills of ——————— and———————.

listening, speaking

9. Since the Language Experience Approach also emphasizes that the learner must recognize that his speech can be recorded in print, the learner's spoken ideas are expressed for him in ——————— form.

printed or written

10. Thus, if a child paints a picture, for example, and expresses the idea of the picture in spoken words, the teacher might then express the child's spoken ideas in ——————— form.

printed or written

11. The teacher might also express in written form any experiences, projects, or other activities which the child might express in ——————— form.

spoken or oral

12. After an appropriate number of similar experiences, the child acquires the concept that written words stand for ——————— words.

oral or spoken

13. The third premise of the Language Experience Approach is that what a child can write or what others can write for him can be ———————.

read

14. Since what is written by a child or for a child is based on the child's personal experiences, and since these experiences are expressed in the child's own vocabulary, any words which the child is called upon to read will be words which are unfamiliar to the child only in their ——————— form.

printed or written

15. If a child's words are unfamiliar to him only in their printed form, repeated instances of exposing a child to his words in their printed form will usually enable him to ——————— the words eventually.

read

16. A child's personal experiences, expressed in his own words, constitute material which is meaning-

ful to him. Learning is enhanced when a learner encounters material which is meaningful to him. Therefore, an apparent advantage in learning to read with the Language Experience Approach is that the learner always encounters material

meaningful

which is _____ to him.

17. If the printed words which a child reads expose him to only those experiences with which he is familiar, the value he might derive from having the opportunity to read about unfamiliar experiences in printed material will be lost. An apparent disadvantage, then, of the Language Experience Approach is that the development of new concepts is not particularly advanced because a child is restricted to reading printed materials which contain experiences with which he is already

familiar

_____.

Review Questions

1. Which three basic premises underlie the Language Experience Approach? (See Frame 6 to check your answer.)

2. Identify one apparent advantage of the Language Experience Approach in teaching beginning reading. (See Frame 16 to check your answer.)

3. Identify one apparent disadvantage of the Language Experience Approach in teaching beginning reading. (See Frame 17 to check your answer.)

PART FIVE: Individualized Reading

OBJECTIVE: The reader will be able to describe the philosophy of the individualized reading approach, to delineate how an individualized reading approach might be initiated, and to state the advantages and limitations of the individualized reading approach.

1. Many activities in teaching are a result of a teacher's attempt to adapt instruction to the needs of each individual child. For example, the activity of assessing readiness or progress, the activity of

grouping for instruction, and even the utilization of a particular approach to teaching reading can be regarded as attempts to adapt instruction to

individual

the needs of each _____ child.

2. When any aspect of instruction is adapted to meet the needs of an individual child, it can be said that that aspect of instruction has been *individualized*. Hence, if a teacher provides a special assignment to meet the needs of a particular child, this aspect of his instruction — assignment-

individualized

making — can be said to be _____.

3. Similarly, when a teacher adopts an instructional approach which is intended to capitalize upon the particular abilities of a given child, it can be said that his instructional approach has been

individualized

_____.

4. There are many factors to consider if instruction is to be individualized. For example, children have differences in interests, differences in abilities, and differences in rates of learning, as well as a multitude of differences in other important characteristics. If a teacher individualizes his instruction to provide for differences in interests only, it is possible that his instruction might not be individualized on the basis of other important

characteristics or
factors

_____.

5. It appears reasonable to conclude then that the greater the number of individual differences which are taken into consideration in providing instruction, the more the instruction can be said

individualized

to be _____.

6. Several approaches to reading instruction have been criticized because of the limited opportunities they provide for individualization. For example, even though teachers' manuals in many basal reading series provide teachers with suggestions for adapting instruction to meet individual differences, often all children are asked to read the same material even though the material

might not be of interest to them. Basal materials, as a result, have been criticized because they do not provide for individual differences in

interest

_____ .

7. Programmed reading, an approach which has been advocated as being highly individualized, has also been criticized because of the limited opportunities provided for individualization. Despite the fact that linear programs are individualized on the basis of the rate at which children progress, they are not individualized on the basis

**characteristics or
factors**

of several other important _____ .

8. It is probable that any approach to reading instruction can be criticized — fairly or unfairly — on the grounds that it excludes one or more important characteristics of children in its provisions for individualization of instruction. One approach which attempts to provide for several kinds of individual differences is *Individualized Reading,* so named because its chief emphasis is on meeting several kinds of individual

differences

_____ among children.

9. In Individualized Reading, the attempt is made to provide each child with the opportunity to seek and select his own reading materials with minimal guidance from the teacher. By providing each child with the opportunity to seek and select his own reading materials from the library or other sources, it is felt that the child will select materials which meet his individual interests and abilities. Individualized Reading, therefore, can be said to

interests

provide for individual differences in _____

abilities

and _____ .

10. After seeking and selecting his own materials, a child is encouraged to proceed at his own rate in reading the materials. Therefore, it can also be said that Individualized Reading provides for in-

rate

dividual differences in _____ of learning.

11. The child's activities of *seeking, self-selection, and pacing* the rate at which he will learn allow

for personal involvement on the part of the learner in planning his instruction, as well as in providing for individualization in interests, general reading ability, and rate. A further attempt at individualization is made through individual conferences held between the child and the teacher. A conference might include reading and discussion of material a child has selected, allowing the teacher to make instructional decisions based on the child's reading of his self-selected

materials   _____.

12. For example, during an individual conference, a teacher might notice that a child is deficient in a particular reading skill. The teacher might provide immediate individualized instruction in the

skill   particular reading _____ and provide small-group instruction at a later time for several children who might need the same skill.

13. In Individualized Reading, instruction in a given skill would occur when the need for the skill became apparent to the teacher. If a child demonstrates no need for a particular skill, the teacher

instruction or practice   would not provide _____ in the skill.

14. Since in Individualized Reading instruction in a specific skill is provided only when a child demonstrates a need for the skill, it can be said that Individualized Reading is individualized not only on the basis of a child's general ability as evidenced by the materials he selects, but also on the basis of his need for instruction in specific

skills   reading _____.

15. The fact that a child is instructed in a specific skill only when the teacher identifies a need for the skill is often cited as an advantage of Individualized Reading. However, it is possible that a teacher might fail to identify a child's need for a

skill   particular _____ and, hence, fail to teach the skill.

16. If a teacher is not knowledgeable concerning the scope and sequence of skills to be taught, or if

a teacher fails to identify a child's need for a particular skill and, as a result, fails to teach the skill, it is possible that important skills could be omitted in reading instruction. Individualization based on the teaching of a reading skill only when a need for the skill is apparent to a teacher might be regarded as an advantage of Individualized Reading. It could also be regarded as a

_____ of Individualized Reading.

disadvantage or limitation

17. Although an advantage of Individualized Reading is that groups are flexible in response to specific skill needs or the sharing of experiences, almost all of the children in a class work at different rates with different materials. Therefore, it is necessary for a teacher to schedule individual conferences. While the individual attention a child receives in an individual conference could be cited as an advantage of Individualized Reading, the minimal amount of time available for conferences with each child could be cited as a

_____ of Individualized Reading.

disadvantage or limitation

18. Since only a minimal amount of time is available for individual conferences, a teacher would probably want to be sure that he would not unnecessarily discuss with a child what might have been discussed during an earlier conference. A substantial amount of record keeping for each child would then be necessary. Teacher time and effort in record keeping might also be cited as a

_____ of Individualized Reading.

disadvantage or limitation

19. Individualized Reading allows a child to read from a wide variety of materials. The opportunity provided to a child to read widely can be identified as still another advantage of this approach. However, the opportunity to select materials from a variety of materials implies that a variety of materials is available. The fact that the providing of a variety of materials might be a financial burden for a school could be regarded as a

_____ of Individualized Reading.

disadvantage or limitation

20. It can be seen that Individualized Reading presents certain advantages as an approach to in-

individual	struction in that it allows for wide latitude in providing for a greater variety of _____ differences among children than do many other approaches to reading instruction.
disadvantages or limitations	21. It can also be seen that in providing for a greater variety of individual differences, however, several problems are encountered which could be cited as _____ of Individualized Reading.
advantages	22. In summary, it can be said that Individualized Reading, like other approaches to reading instruction, presents certain _____ and certain
disadvantages or limitations	_____. The strengths of Individualized Reading appear to lie primarily in the opportunities for seeking, self-selection, and pacing, thereby providing for the meeting of a variety
individual	of _____ differences among children. The limitations of Individualized Reading appear to lie in the problems encountered in attempting
differences	to provide for individual _____ among children.

Review Questions

1. What are the possible advantages of Individualized Reading as an approach to reading instruction? (See Frames 15-22 to check your answer.)

2. Under what conditions could the advantages of Individualized Reading become disadvantages? (See Frames 15-22 to check your answer.)

PART SIX: The Linguistic Approach

OBJECTIVE: The reader will be able to define terminology associated with the linguistic approach, and describe the advantages and disadvantages of the linguistic approach.

1. *Linguistics* is commonly defined as the scientific study of a language. A scholar who becomes pro-

linguistic

ficient in the use of a language and who understands the many facets of that language can be properly called a ―――――― scientist.

2. A segment of the study of a language is a scientific study of its speech sounds. Linguists who attempt to apply their knowledge of speech sounds to printed language for the purpose of teaching others to read that printed language are setting

linguistic

forth a ―――――― approach to reading instruction.

3. Linguistics, like many areas of research, has its own vocabulary for some common understandings. In the next few frames, you will be introduced to a few of the terms that make up the

vocabulary

―――――― of linguistics.

4. *Phoneme* is a linguistic term; it is a unit of speech sounds, the smallest unit of speech sound in a language. There are about forty-three or forty-four such sound units in the English language.

phoneme

Each of these sound units is called a ――――――.

5. *Grapheme* is a linguistic term used to designate the symbol that represents in *printed* language the phoneme in *spoken* language. Single letters and groups of letters represent phonemes in the English language; these symbols are called

graphemes

――――――.

6. Another common linguistic term is *phonemic-graphemic correspondence*. This term is used to refer to the *agreement of a speech sound with the letter or group of letters that represents it* in printed language. For example, the sound represented by the letter *a* in the word *cat* is the same as the sound represented by the letter *a* in the

phonemic-
graphemic

word *pad*. In this example, there is a ――――――-

―――――― correspondence (or agreement) between the printed letter (grapheme) *a* and the sound (phoneme) it represents in the words *cat* and *pad*.

7. Among linguists there is lack of agreement regarding how reading is to be taught. However, there have emerged some procedures and characteristics that appear somewhat common to the linguistic reading programs now on the market.

procedures
characteristics

The following frames will present _____

and _____ found to be common in published linguistic reading programs.

8. The initial procedure is to have *students learn the names of the letters* of the alphabet. A number of techniques and activities have been suggested for accomplishing this; for example, some programs recommend that the alphabet song be sung. A child can be said to know the alphabet when, upon being presented a letter in either its small or capital form, he can name that

letter

_____ of the alphabet.

9. Another procedure is to present phonemic-graphemic correspondence to students in *words that fit a basic spelling pattern.* The first pattern is usually the consonant-vowel-consonant pattern, the C-V-C pattern. The medial vowel in this pattern represents the short sound of the vowel. In the word *sit,* the vowel *i* is between the two consonants *s* and *t.* In the word "sit," the letter

short

i represents its _____ sound.

10. To learn a new word that fits a certain spelling pattern, the student will be asked to spell the word from left to right. The teacher will then spell the word and pronounce it. Then the child will be asked to pronounce the word. Words, similar in pattern, will be presented in the same manner. This procedure is to *lead a child to the eventual recognition of the basic spelling pattern* and,

words

therefore, to read other _____ that fit the pattern.

11. Linguistic reading programs *do not usually direct students to say, in isolation, the sound that a letter represents* in a word. In a word that fits the C-V-C spelling pattern (*hat,* for example), a child

sound

would not be asked to say, in isolation, the
———————— that *h* stands for.

12. As a student progresses in a linguistic reading program, several new spelling patterns will be presented. Each new pattern is likely to be progressively more complex and proportionately less frequently used in material printed in the English language. Although each succeeding spelling pattern presented to the student is still a basic pattern, the printed material a child reads will furnish

pattern

him less opportunity to use the ————————, for it appears less frequently than the earlier patterns presented.

13. Because a certain word may be needed before the pattern in which it fits has been presented or because the word fits no basic spelling pattern, the word is presented as a *sight (irregular)* word. Take the word *the* as an example. To read the sentence, "The fat cat sat," a student will be told how to pronounce the word *the*. Because the word *the* fits no pattern yet presented, it

sight or irregular

is presented to the student as a ————————
word.

14. Another procedure common to the linguistic approach in the early stages is to *deemphasize* activities that dwell on developing *meaning of what is read.* It is assumed that students at the beginning stage of reading have sizable listening and speaking vocabularies. The major task in reading, therefore, is to translate the printed word back into speech. When this is accomplished, the child is expected to know the

meaning

———————— of what he has read.

15. In addition, the linguistic programs *take a rather "dim" view of the use of pictures as an aid to identifying words that are strange in print.* Some programs eliminate all pictures from the early readers; others may decorate pages with designs that are colorful but unrelated to the meaning of the selection being read. In reading programs of

this approach, a person would not expect to find pictures or illustrations to be used as aids to

identifying

_____ strange printed words.

16. A characteristic of linguistic reading programs is the extreme *contrast between* the quality of the *earliest material* the student is asked to read *and the material that follows* a few months later. Typical of an early story is the following:

Pat the Cat

Pat is a cat.
Pat can run.
Run, Pat.
Run to the bun.
Run to the sun.
Run to the red,
    red sun.
To run is fun.

The sample story utilizes the basic C-V-C spelling pattern. The quality of the story is obviously curtailed because of its being limited to this basic

pattern

spelling _____.

17. In a surprisingly few months, the students being instructed in a linguistic reading program are exposed to stories of rather exceptional literary quality and difficulty. It is believed that once students have been presented the various basic spelling patterns and the needed sight words they will be prepared to "tackle" with success and interest material of considerable difficulty and of

quality

high literary _____.

18. Many published linguistic reading programs extend only through the second year of instruction. A few have complete programs that extend upward through the elementary school. For a school system that adopts a linguistic reading program, it will likely be necessary for it to determine what later reading program will be most effective for the students who initially receive instruction in

linguistic

a _____ reading program.

19. There are many approaches to teaching beginning reading. An approach that incorporates the

linguistic

knowledge of the speech sounds of a language in scientific manner is called the _____ approach.

20. Several linguistic terms are used in the linguistic approach to reading. Units of speech sounds are

phonemes

called _____; the symbol that repre-

grapheme

sents a sound unit is called a _____;

and the association that exists between a speech sound and its printed symbol is called

phonemic-graphemic
    correspondence

_____-_____ _____.

21. Phonemic-graphemic correspondences are pre-

patterns

sented to students in basic spelling _____ common in printed English words.

22. English words that do not fit a basic spelling pattern, yet are needed by the student at a par-

sight

ticular time, are presented as _____ (or irregular) words.

Review Questions

1. What is the study of linguistics? (See Frame 1 to check your answer.)

2. What terms are commonly used in linguistic reading programs? (See Frames 4-6 and/or 20 to check your answer.)

3. List procedures and characteristics commonly found in linguistic reading programs. (See Frames 8, 9, 11, 13, 14, 15, and 17 to check your answer.)

PART SEVEN: The "Systems" Approach

OBJECTIVE: The reader will be able to name the four main components of a systems approach, and state the difference between an assessment test and a mastery test.

1. Lesson One in this text delineated commonly accepted reading skills in the areas of word attack, comprehension, and reading study skills. A group of experienced reading teachers, if provided with

sufficient time to discuss what a person needs to know in learning to read, would probably reach

skills

agreement on a similar set of _____ essential to a person's learning to read.

2. The same group of teachers would be less likely to come to an agreement as to a best method to use in teaching these skills or the best materials

skills

to use in teaching these _____.

3. Although teachers might well agree on the skills to be taught in developing a reader, it is far less

method

likely they will reach agreement on a _____

materials

of teaching these skills or on the best _____ to use in teaching these skills.

4. An approach to teaching reading that is based upon the idea that it can be determined *what* is to be taught but not *how* or *with what* instructional materials the skills in reading can best be taught has been classified as a *systems approach*

systems

to teaching reading. A _____ approach to teaching reading sets forth what skills are to be taught but not necessarily how or with what

materials or
methods

instructional _____ the skills are to be taught.

5. A systems approach to teaching reading commonly consists of four components. The first component is a *list of* the *skills* to be taught. It is customary for the skills to be sequenced and set forth as behavioral objectives. Reading skills to be taught in a systems approach are commonly

behavioral

set forth in the form of _____ objectives. (See Lesson Seven, Part One.)

6. The second component of a systems approach to teaching reading is the *testing* component. Test items are developed to measure each behavioral

second

objective. Testing is the _____ component

systems

objective

> of a _____ approach to teaching reading. Each test item is developed to measure a behav-
>
> ioral _____.

7. The testing component of a systems approach usually consists of tests for two purposes — assessment and mastery. Assessment tests are administered to students before instruction takes place to determine what skills are already possessed by the student. A test administered to a student previous to instruction in a skill is termed

assessment

> an _____ test.

8. Mastery tests are administered to students after instruction in a reading skill has been taught to determine if the skill has been learned. The test administered to a student after a skill has been taught in the systems approach is termed a

mastery

> _____ test.

9. Both assessment and mastery tests commonly used in a systems approach are criterion-referenced type tests. An arbitrary score (usually between 80% and 90%) is set for determining if mastery by the student has been achieved. Assessment of reading skills already possessed by a student and mastery of skills taught the student are

criterion

> measured by a type of test called a _____ -referenced test.

10. The third component of a systems approach to teaching reading is the teacher's *resource file*. When developed, the resource file will contain a listing of resources that can be used in teaching the reading skills and suggestions for how to teach the reading skills. A file containing a listing of materials to use in teaching a reading skill and suggestions for how to teach the skills are re-

resource

> ferred to as a teacher's _____ file.

11. The teacher's resource file is to be developed locally. Publishers of a systems approach may suggest possible resources for use in teaching the

skills, but it is expected that the actual resource file will be developed at the local school level. Although a published systems approach may make initial suggestions of resources to use in teaching the reading skills set forth in the system, the actual teacher's resource file is expected to

local

be developed at the _____ school level.

12. Materials for the teacher's resource file can be selected from those produced commercially or can be teacher-made materials. The purpose of the resource file is to have readily available the best material to use in the most effective way to meet the needs of the individual student. Materials in the resource file may be commercially

teacher-made

produced or _____. When selecting material from the resource file, it should be done so with the purpose of meeting the needs of the

individual

_____ student.

13. The teacher's resource file should be well organized but maintained in looseleaf form. It is to be expected that materials and ideas for teaching a reading skill will be added to and subtracted from the file as teachers find that some are more or less effective in working with students. Because materials and ideas for teaching may prove to be more or less effective when used with learners, it is recommended that the teacher's resource file be well organized but maintained

looseleaf

in _____ form.

14. The fourth major component of a systems approach to teaching reading is *record keeping*. This is a means of informing teachers about which students have or have not mastered which reading skills. In order for teachers to know which skills have or have not been mastered by which students, it is essential to develop a

record keeping

method of _____ _____.

15. It is from the information kept on the records that teachers group students for instruction in specific

reading skills. Only those students who have not mastered a skill are grouped for instruction in the skill. One chief purpose for keeping records on skills mastered by students is to determine

grouped

which students need to be _____ for instruction on a skill.

16. Record-keeping devices differ among systems approaches on the market today. However, each one attempts to make it relatively easy to determine what skills have or have not been mastered by which students. Although methods of record keeping vary among the systems approaches, the purpose of each is to keep the teachers informed as to which skills have or have not been mastered

student(s)

by which _____.

17. Systems approaches to teaching reading have also been labeled "management approaches." Although they do not specify just what materials should be used in teaching a skill or direct the teacher as to just how to teach a skill, the system

skills

does specify what _____ are to be taught.

18. Criterion-referenced tests are provided by the systems approach. Those administered before

assessment

instruction in a skill are called _____ tests.

19. Criterion-referenced tests administered to students following instruction in a skill are called

mastery

_____ tests.

20. A student is considered to have mastered a read-

80-90

ing skill when he gets between _____% of the test items correct.

21. Teachers decide how to teach a skill and what materials to use in teaching the skill by selecting

teacher's

material: nd ideas from the _____

resource

_____ file.

22. A method of record keeping enables the teacher to be informed as to which skills have or have not

mastered

been _____ by which students.

23. Before administering the tests, building a re-source file, and keeping records, however, a teacher using a systems approach would consult the first component of a systems approach, the

list, skills

_____ of _____ to be taught.

Review Questions

1. What is the difference between an assessment test and a mastery test? (See Frames 7 and 8 to check your answer.)

2. Name the four main components of a Systems Approach. (See Frames 5, 6, 10, and 14 to check your answer.)

BIBLIOGRAPHY

The following sources provide comprehensive presentations of the concepts initiated in this book:

Aukerman, Robert C. *Approaches to Beginning Reading.* New York: John Wiley and Sons, Inc., 1971.

Burns, Paul C., and Roe, Betty D. *Teaching Reading in Today's Elementary Schools.* Chicago: Rand McNally College Publishing Company, 1976.

Burron, Arnold, and Claybaugh, Amos L. *Using Reading to Teach Subject Matter.* Columbus, Ohio: Charles E. Merrill Publishing Company, 1974.

Bush, Clifford L., and Huebner, Mildred H. *Strategies for Reading in the Elementary School.* London: The Macmillan Company, 1970.

Chall, Jeanne S. *Learning to Read: The Great Debate.* New York: McGraw-Hill Book Company, 1967.

Dallmann, Martha; Rouch, Roger C.; Chang, Lynette Y.C.; and De Boer, John J. *The Teaching of Reading,* 4th ed. New York: Holt, Rinehart and Winston, Inc., 1974.

Durkin, Dolores. *Teaching Them to Read,* 2nd ed. Boston: Allyn and Bacon, Inc., 1974.

Ekwall, Eldon. *Locating and Correcting Reading Difficulties.* Columbus, Ohio: Charles E. Merrill Publishing Company, 1970.

Farr, Roger. *Measurement and Evaluation of Reading.* New York: Harcourt Brace Jovanovich, Inc., 1970.

Gallant, Ruth. *Handbook in Corrective Reading: Basic Tasks.* Columbus, Ohio: Charles E. Merrill Publishing Company, 1970.

Harris, Albert J., and Sipay, Edward R. *Effective Teaching of Reading.* New York: David McKay Company, Inc., 1971.

Heilman, Arthur W. *Phonics in Proper Perspective,* 3rd ed. Columbus, Ohio: Charles E. Merrill Publishing Company, 1976.

——————. *Principles and Practices of Teaching Reading,* 3rd ed. Columbus, Ohio: Charles E. Merrill Publishing Company, 1972.

Kibler, Robert J.; Barker, Larry L.; and Miles, David T. *Behavioral Objectives and Instruction.* Boston: Allyn and Bacon, Inc., 1970.

Kottmeyer, William. *Decoding and Meaning: A Modest Proposal.* New York: McGraw-Hill Book Company, 1974.

McKee, Paul, and Durr, William K. *Reading: A Program of Instruction for the Elementary School.* Boston: Houghton Mifflin Company, 1966.

Otto, Wayne, and Chester, Robert D. *Objective-Based Reading.* Reading, Mass.: Addison-Wesley Publishing Company, 1976.

Otto, Wayne; Chester, Robert D.; McNeil, John; and Myers, Shirley. *Focused Reading Instruction.* Reading, Mass.: Addison-Wesley Publishing Company, 1974.

Robeck, Mildred Coen, and Wilson, John A.R. *Psychology of Reading.* New York: John Wiley and Sons, Inc., 1974.

Smith, Richard J., and Johnson, Dale D. *Teaching Children to Read.* Reading, Mass.: Addison-Wesley Publishing Company, 1976.

Spache, George D., and Spache, Evelyn B. *Reading in the Elementary School,* 3rd ed. Boston: Allyn and Bacon, Inc., 1973.

Stauffler, Russell G. *Directing the Reading Thinking Process.* New York: Harper and Row, Publishers, 1975.

Veatch, Jeannette. *Reading in the Elementary School.* New York: The Ronald Press Company, 1966.

Wilson, Robert M., and Hall, Maryanne. *Programmed Word Attack for Teachers,* 2nd ed. Columbus, Ohio: Charles E. Merrill Publishing Company, 1974.

————. *Reading and the Elementary School Child.* New York: D. Van Nostrand Company, 1972.

Zintz, Miles V. *The Reading Process,* 2nd ed. Dubuque, Iowa: William C. Brown Company, Publishers, 1975.